Secrets of the Nanny Whisperer

A PERIGEE BOOK
Published by the Penguin Group
Penguin Group (USA) LLC
375 Hudson Street, New York, New York 10014

USA • Canada • UK • Ireland • Australia • New Zealand • India • South Africa • China

penguin.com

A Penguin Random House Company

Library of Congress Cataloging-in-Publication Data

Gold, Tammy.
Secrets of the nanny whisperer : a practical guide for finding and achieving the gold standard of care for
your child / by Tammy Gold.— First edition.
pages   cm
ISBN 978-0-399-16988-5 (paperback)
1. Nannies—Employment—United States.   2. Nannies—Selection and appointment—United States.
3. Child care services—United States.   I. Title.
HQ778.63.G645   2015
649'.10973—dc23   2014040010

First edition: January 2015

PRINTED IN THE UNITED STATES OF AMERICA

10 9 8 7 6 5 4 3 2 1

Text design by Kristin del Rosario

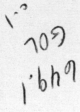

Secrets of the Nanny Whisperer

A Practical Guide for Finding and Achieving
the Gold Standard of Care for Your Child

Tammy Gold, LCSW, MSW, LSW, CEC

A PERIGEE BOOK

To my husband, Jason,
and our daughters, Braydin, Presley, and Gemma

There is no book big enough, no dedication long enough,
and no words possible that could ever express the intense
love I feel for all of you, the insane joy you bring me,
and the daily gratitude I feel to be the mommy of our family.

Every good deed in my life came back to me
in the four of you . . .

CONTENTS

INTRODUCTION

·————·

How I Became the Nanny Whisperer

Welcome to *Secrets of the Nanny Whisperer*. My name is Tammy Gold, and today is the day that finding the perfect nanny for your family just got easier. Whether you're a first-time parent or a mother of five, whether you work seventy hours a week or twenty, hiring someone to help you care for your most precious possession—your child—can be an incredibly daunting task. The good news is that it no longer has to be. You've picked up this book, and I'm here to help.

In many ways, my life has always been about helping parents and their children. After college, I received my master's degree in social work from Columbia University and began working as a therapist for at-risk children in a New Jersey school. It was while working with these kids—many of whom suffered from neglect and abuse—that I witnessed firsthand the effects that poor caregiving could have on a child and the critical link between healthy, effective parenting and a child's social, emotional, and intellectual development.

As a student at Columbia, I had been very interested in attachment theory, which is the science of how early caregiving influences a child's life. First developed by the British psychiatrist John Bowlby, attachment theory asserts that for an infant's social and emotional development to occur normally, the child needs to form a close, trusting relationship with at least one primary caregiver during infancy and the earliest years of life. Other well-known theorists such as Mary Ainsworth and Erik Erikson confirmed Bowlby's research with a number of landmark studies that showed conclusively that the earliest bonds formed by children with their caregivers have a tremendous impact. A mother who is available and responsive to an infant's needs establishes a sense of security and creates what Ainsworth called a "secure base" for the child to then explore the world. Erikson argued that a child's entire identity is shaped by an early sense of "trust vs. mistrust," depending on whether his caregivers reliably respond to his needs and provide constant care and affection. In short, infants and very young children *need* to establish strong relationships with loving, devoted caregivers in order to grow up to be emotionally healthy, happy, stable adults.

It was also around this time that I gave birth to our first daughter, Braydin. After years of dreaming about having my own children, motherhood didn't turn out to be as easy or straightforward as I'd expected. Braydin was extremely colicky, so instead of sharing all of these beautiful Pampers moments with my new baby, she cried constantly, and I was a wreck. The pediatrician had no answers, and I just kept thinking to myself, "How is it possible that I had no preparation for this?" I was exhausted and overwhelmed, and worst of all, I felt like I was failing as a parent. Here I was, a childhood therapist, and I had no idea how to help my own child!

Eventually, through my own research, I figured out that Braydin had reflux, and once I switched her to a hypoallergenic formula, she was a new baby. But the experience made me realize that all parents occasionally need help to be the best caregivers they can be—even those, like myself, who have experience with children. When my maternity leave ended, I decided to start my own business devoted to giving moms and dads the support and tools they need to be better parents, particularly in the early, developmentally crucial years of a child's life. Because I had studied attachment theory and child development, I knew that there was, in fact, an essential formula for raising happy, well-adjusted children. I wanted to share this information with other parents, so I started taking on clients and the business grew.

But then something unexpected started to happen. I was working from home and had hired a nanny, Maria, to care for Braydin while I was with my clients. After those first rough months with a colicky baby, Maria was a godsend. She was warm and lively and full of energy, always willing to jump in and do whatever was needed. She was fantastic with Braydin, always singing and playing and loving, and she was a huge support for me as well while I learned to juggle motherhood and my career. Even my friends noticed that Maria was providing our family with a whole different level of childcare, and they started asking me, "How did you find your nanny? I've never seen a nanny like that before." Or saying, "I wish I had a relationship with my nanny like the one you have with Maria," because they saw that there was no tension or drama. Before long, they approached me to ask for help, saying, "I know this isn't exactly what you do, but what we really need more than anything is a good nanny. Can you help us find someone like Maria?"

So I started helping my friends find their nannies, and I quickly learned that I approached the nanny-search process very differently from other parents. Most of them treated it like hiring a babysitter, and if the nanny could answer basic questions and had good references, they made an offer. But when I had hired Maria, I had instinctively employed all my skills as a social worker and therapist—that is, the ability to read people and assess their character and personality, as well as perform a candid self-assessment—to help me figure out the right fit for our family. I had used my knowledge of child development theory to think about what Braydin needed most at the time, and when I met with nanny candidates, my therapist training allowed me to pick up on subtle cues and spot red flags that most people didn't see. I also realized that my relationship with Maria had directly benefited from my experience as a therapist working with both individuals and couples; by using proper communication techniques, I had been able to foster an extremely positive working relationship between us while at the same time motivating her to perform at a high level. Soon, in addition to helping my friends find great caregivers, I was being invited into their homes to help them communicate more effectively with their nannies and mend broken nanny–family relationships. I found myself on the front lines of the nanny–parent experience, gaining unique insights and information, and learning how to make the relationship work for both parties at every stage.

I also realized that the best childcare situations were defined by what I call Constancy of Care—that is, a marked continuity in terms of quality and style of care across *all* caregivers who are responsible for the child: mother, father, and nanny, as well as any babysitters or daycare workers. If the nanny was able to mirror the parents in terms of attentiveness and parenting approach, the child was always calm and happy, even when the parents left, because she never experienced a drop in the level of care or affection. By finding a nanny who was able to parent "like Mom," or teaching the current nanny to mimic the parents' caregiving style, mothers and fathers could be apart from their children while still creating the stability and close, consistent emotional bonds promoted by attachment theory. Helping parents achieve their own particular version of Constancy of Care, both during and after the hiring process, became a key part of my Gold Standard approach.

As time went on, and the word of mouth spread, my friends started calling me the "Nanny Whisperer," and I decided to offer nanny–family matching and mediation as official services through my business. My first paying client was a new mom, Natalie, who worked in Manhattan and was about to leave her six-week-old daughter to go back to work. And it was through helping her that I truly understood just how life-changing these services could be. Here was this new mother, so vulnerable and overwhelmed and terrified of leaving her child. But when together we found her a wonderful caregiver, it made all the difference. She felt so much better about herself as a mom and about the life choices she had made because she was confident that her daughter would be getting the very best possible care while she was gone.

How to Use This Book

Whether you are about to hire a nanny for the very first time, or you currently employ a nanny, this book can help you improve your experience and achieve the Gold Standard of care for your child. Part 1 explains my approach and why the right family–nanny match is so important. It also introduces you to my unique way of thinking about nannies and childcare, so that you can truly understand what a nanny is and does and what you should expect from the relationship. It also explores the common myths and misconceptions about nannies that create problems between parents and their child's caregiver. Part 2 presents my Gold Standard hiring process, which is designed to help you find your ideal nanny and includes my one-of-a-kind Family Needs Assessment as well as breakthrough approaches to screening, reference checks, interviews, and doing in-home trials.

Part 3 is all about managing the relationship with your nanny and resolving any issues or conflicts that may arise. If you already have a nanny but aren't completely satisfied and aren't sure whether you should stick with your current caregiver or start fresh, Part 3 is designed to help you bring out the best in your nanny and know which issues are fixable and which are a sign that it's time to move on. Every child deserves the Gold Standard of care, and you have everything you need in these pages to achieve that exceptional standard of care in your own home.

In the years since I became the Nanny Whisperer, I have learned that what I do to help families is incredibly important. When I place a great nanny or mend an existing nanny–parent relationship, something magical happens. I've helped the mom be a better mother because she now has a true partner—she can be "on" with her children and then leave for work or go recharge at the gym or have coffee with friends, knowing that her child is in great hands. I've helped the dad because he can pursue his job with peace of mind, and I've helped their marriage by giving them both more time and energy to devote to each other. And I've helped the children the most because they're being cared for not just by capable parents but by an extra capable adult as well—and everyone's happy! Happy parents and a happy caregiver make for a double-happy child.

So how do we get you and your family to this happy place? Let's get started.

PART ONE

Nanny Whisperer 101

CHAPTER 1

———

The Quest for the Perfect Nanny

How (and How Not) to Achieve
the Gold Standard of Care

One afternoon at one of my "Nanny Know-How" events in New York City, a young woman stood up and introduced herself to the group.

"Hi, my name is Karen," she began. "And I just wanted to say that I am the poster child for how not to go about finding a nanny.

"Our daughter is six months old, and we started looking for a nanny, which was our first choice for childcare, several months ago. We thought we had plenty of time before I had to go back to work, but now I'm actually starting back at work next week, and our daughter is going to daycare because we never found the right person. We went about our search in completely the wrong way; we didn't really know what we wanted, so we just started bringing people in and talking to them, thinking that we'd have an emotional connection with someone and that would mean everything else was right. We didn't understand how uncomfortable talking about money would be, so we met with a ton of nannies without really discussing salary, and then when we finally found someone we liked, she said she wanted to be paid 'off the books.' We wanted to do 'on the books,' so after all that legwork, we couldn't agree on salary and the nanny took another job.

"Now our daughter is starting daycare and I have to do the nanny search all over again. I'm here because, this time, I want to do it right."

I immediately understood Karen's experience, because it is typical of the way that most parents choose nannies: They feel their way through this most important process without a plan, and with only their gut instincts to guide them. But finding a nanny is no small task, and more parents face this challenge today than ever before. Whether you are East Coast or West Coast, urban or suburban, chances are that many of the parents that you know rely on some form of regular childcare. The number of families with two working parents continues to grow, and even moms and dads who chose to be at home or at home part-time often require an extra set of hands to keep up with the pace and demands of modern parenthood. In fact, statistics show that 50 percent of all U.S. children are in some type of formal childcare arrangement by the time they are nine months old. Finding the right person (or persons) to care for your child when you are not there has become every bit as essential as potty training and teaching the ABCs.

Yet while there are hundreds of resources available to tell you how to puree your own organic baby food or sleep train your toddler, there are almost none that teach moms and dads the right way to go about finding a nanny, or how to work with that nanny effectively. Many of my clients come to me as first-time parents because they are completely daunted by the nanny-search process—where to find a nanny, what to expect, and how much to pay—but I also get clients who, despite the best of intentions, have been through five nannies in two years and have no idea what they're doing wrong. Most parents rely on advice from friends when conducting their search, but without a proven system or strategy to guide them, they end up making mistakes that set the stage for future problems: They prioritize the wrong qualifications, ask the wrong questions, and fail to zero in on what they, as a family, truly need. It doesn't help that the nanny world is like the Wild West, completely unregulated and often under the table; there are no rules, there is no standardized training or hiring protocol, and there is no board or government agency to provide professional oversight. Anyone can advertise themselves as a nanny, and yet I have found that many parents do more due diligence when buying a car than they do when hiring their child's caregiver.

Unfortunately, the stakes are higher than they realize. Science tells us that 90 percent of the human brain develops by age three, so any person who cares for your child during these formative years—be it a nanny, a babysitter, or a daycare worker—will without question shape your child's personality. Young children, especially infants and toddlers, learn from their caregivers every minute of every day, which means that everything about your nanny—her demeanor, her physicality, and whether or not she will actively teach and engage your child—will have a direct impact on his or her social, emotional, and intellectual development. If the chemistry between the nanny and child isn't right, if the nanny is bored or checked out, if there is high nanny turnover, or if the nanny–parent relationship is strained, there can be real and lasting consequences for the child. Especially during the early years, the difference between an exceptional caregiver and a mediocre one can be enormous.

That's why I wrote this book. After years of working with families and their nannies, I have created what I call the Gold Standard process so that parents everywhere can finally have a surefire prescription for finding their perfect nanny and making a lasting match that will help their child thrive. No matter who you are, where you live, or what kind of nanny you're looking for, this book gives you everything you need to achieve the Gold Standard of childcare: a loving, energetic, totally devoted caregiver who is ideally matched—both personally and professionally—to meet your unique needs and those of your child. My hiring process will allow you to take control, avoid mistakes, and hire the right person. And if you already employ a nanny and it isn't perfect, the strategies in this book—based on my background in psychotherapy as well as my experience as a nanny–family mediator—can help you improve the situation and achieve a whole new level of success.

Starting today, I want you to set aside whatever you think you know about how to hire a great nanny. Forget what you've read online or what your friends have told you, because I can tell you from experience that most of the typical nanny-search methods don't work. Many parents, like Karen, approach the process backward: They round up a random assortment of nannies referred to them by friends and friends of friends, interview the nannies first, decide which ones they like, and then try to figure out who can match their actual, logistical needs. Or they do what I call Nanny Speed-Dating: They pick a day, invite ten candidates to meet them at Starbucks, interview each one for an hour, and then hire the person they like best. I also know plenty of parents who don't even bother to interview multiple candidates—they just hire the cousin of their best friend's nanny, or a neighbor's former nanny, because they don't want to bother with an extensive search.

Unfortunately, all of these approaches are rife with pitfalls. The problem with the interview-first approach, as Karen learned, is that it wastes a lot of time. Unless you figure out your exact needs and job criteria at the outset, you will spend a lot of energy meeting with candidates who ultimately, for one reason or another, aren't right for the job. No parent—especially an exhausted parent with a newborn—wants to spend any more time on their nanny search than is absolutely necessary. But if you try to rush things, as with Nanny Speed-Dating, you are not going to be able to gather sufficient information about each candidate to truly assess them and make the smartest choice for your family. Even referrals are not a sure bet: As many parents will tell you, referrals may mean a lot—or they may mean nothing. Just because a nanny was wonderful for your friend does not automatically mean she will be wonderful for you. You need far more information than can be gleaned from a single interview, a single day of meeting nannies, or a single reference to know whether a nanny is right for you and your child.

Avoiding the wrong match is also critically important. There are many mediocre and even bad nannies out there who will meet you armed with years of experience and decent references. Mediocre nannies often fly under the radar, and the truth is that many parents don't actually know what their nannies are doing all day long while they're at work. There are many supposedly good nannies who commit what I call "benign neglect"—that is, they do the physical aspects of the job, such as feeding and dressing, but neglect the emotional ones, such as playing, interacting, and being affectionate with the child. Nanny searches are tricky, because you're not only trying to find the good nannies—you're also trying to identify and weed out the bad ones.

Fortunately, that's where I come in. Because I have worked with hundreds of parents and been present for all of their nanny-search ups and downs, I know what works and what doesn't when it comes to making a successful match. The Gold Standard hiring process described in Part 2 takes all of my firsthand experience combined with psychological research and translates it into a proven system for finding a great nanny. If you have made mistakes in the past, don't worry! My process is designed to help you attain the very highest quality of care—the Gold Standard of care—for your child.

The process starts with a detailed Family Needs Assessment, which draws on my background in psychotherapy and child development to help you to identify your wants and your needs. We then translate those needs into an actual job description, and use four key points of interaction—Basic Screening, Reference Checks, Interviews, and Trials—to match that description to a strategically selected pool of candidates who have a high probability of being exactly what you want. While many parents do these steps in some form already, the way we approach them is unique. The sequencing of the steps is also very important; for example, we do reference checks before meeting candidates face to face, because I know from experience that when the check is done correctly, what you can learn from former employers is far more telling than an interview.

I've had clients say to me, "Wow, your process is like a science!" I take that as a compliment, because the whole point of my methodology is that, when done correctly, it yields a predictable result. You owe it to yourself and your child to set the bar high, and that's what this book is about. You can find your perfect nanny by following my plan.

Now that you understand why the process is so important, let's learn about the other side of this match: the nannies.

———•———

CHAPTER 2

Nannyology

*Understanding Nannies
and How They Work*

One day, I received a call from a woman named Alicia, who lived in Connecticut with her husband, John. She had recently given birth to their first child, and with only three weeks left on her maternity leave, she was faced with the task of hiring her first nanny.

"I'm stressed because I have no idea what I'm doing," she told me. "I don't know what I'm looking for, or where to begin. And I'm nervous because I didn't grow up with a nanny. I don't understand nannies, and I don't even really want a nanny in my house—but I have to go back to work. Can you help me?"

Many of my clients are first-time parents who come to me feeling a lot like Alicia. They're anxious because even though they want to hire a nanny, they don't know much about them, so they don't know where to start. The nanny world can be confusing and mysterious: Nannies can be as different as night and day, and there's no nanny degree or required certification. Parents are forced to make up the rules on the fly in their own homes, and as a result, they often have misguided notions or expectations about what a nanny should or shouldn't be. It doesn't help that for many of us, the nanny we're most familiar with is Mary Poppins—so we envision spoonfuls of sugar and everyone living happily ever after and are disappointed when a real-world nanny fails to measure up. However, I can assure you that there are many, many wonderful nannies out there who, even if they don't travel via umbrella, can be immensely loved by both you and your child, contribute to the joys of family life, and enhance your perspective on childrearing in remarkable ways. But first, you'll need a good understanding of who they are, how they think, and what to expect from the arrangement.

> We envision spoonfuls of sugar and everyone living happily ever after.

This chapter is designed to give you an introduction to what I call "Nannyology"—the science of understanding nannies—and to give you a crystal-clear picture of what a nanny is and does, what the job actually entails, and how you should and should *not* approach the relationship. Nannies are human, and just like everyone else, they have strengths and weaknesses, surprising talents and funny quirks, and their own needs and expectations. You will most likely never find the perfect nanny who flawlessly performs every conceivable task. However, if you follow my hiring process and the strategies for working together that are detailed later in the book, you can absolutely find an amazing, real-world nanny who will be a great fit for your family.

A nanny is someone who cares for a child or children in a home on a regular basis during the parents' absence. Nannies are usually responsible for everything to do with the care of the child, including feeding, bathing, sleep scheduling, laundry, and tidying up the child's room or play areas. Nannies may also have additional responsibilities that help the family, such as errands, grocery shopping, cooking for the children, caring for pets, and light housekeeping. A full-time nanny will typically work forty to sixty hours a week, and part-time nanny may work anywhere from fifteen to thirty-five.

The biggest advantage to having a nanny is that your child will be cared for by a consistent, attentive caregiver in the familiar surroundings of your home. Aside from having a family member to care for your child, a nanny most closely approximates a parent, and depending on your situation, she may do everything that a parent does—from helping with homework to settling sibling disputes—when you're not there. A nanny also gives parents maximum flexibility: You get to decide what hours and duties you need and then hire someone who fits the bill. Many nannies will even work extra weekend hours or travel with you on family vacations. The consistency and stability that a good nanny provides is ideal for young children, especially babies and toddlers, and in the best scenarios, the nanny becomes a member of your family who loves your children as if they were her own.

The downside is that nannies are by far the most expensive form of childcare. The average rate is $15 per hour, or $700 a week, depending on where you live, and the price goes up with each additional child. Like most employees, nannies expect a modest annual raise (50 cents an hour, or $25 a week) along with paid vacation days, sick days, personal days, and holidays. It is also considered good practice to give your nanny a bonus at the end of the calendar year (typically one to two weeks' salary) or on her yearly anniversary with you.

The other factor to consider is that the nanny–parent relationship, while it can be rewarding in many ways, is utterly unique and not always easy. Even if you and your children adore your nanny, it can be strange to have another adult in your house so many hours a week and even stranger to hear that adult express authoritative opinions about your children and what they need. Most parents, even those who really like or even love their nannies, have a certain amount of ambivalence about the relationship, and it can be challenging to constantly walk the line between personal and professional, family member and employee. Negotiating that line comes with the territory, and when you hire a nanny, you will need to devote time and energy to the relationship (more about this in Part 3).

The Different Types of Nannies

There are many different types of nannies, and which kind you hire will depend on factors specific to your household, including the ages and number of the children, where your family lives, whether you and your partner both work full-time, and whether you employ any other domestic help. These various types include live-in and live-out, urban and suburban, as well as specific kinds of nannies that are further defined by their job duties and responsibilities. Let's take a closer look at each of these types, and at how you will need to think about them as an employer.

LIVE-IN VS. LIVE-OUT

The first big decision that you will need to make when starting to think about who you want to hire is whether your nanny should be live-in or live-out. A live-in nanny is one who lives with the family in their home for some portion of the week, while a live-out nanny commutes to work each day and, after finishing her duties, returns home each night.

Live-In

Live-in nannies can be the least expensive kind of nanny because you are giving them room and board in addition to their salary. Some live-ins go home for some portion of the week, and some stay with their employer's family full-time because they don't have another residence. A typical work schedule for a live-in is five full days and nights on, and two days off each week. If you want additional days and hours, you will need to pay for the extra time. The big advantage of a live-in nanny is that you know you have round-the-clock coverage for those five days: If you and your spouse both travel for work, you have someone to spend the night; if your child is up all night with a stomach virus, you have someone on hand to help; and your nanny will never be late for work because of a snowstorm or the train broke down.

To have a live-in, you need to be able to provide her with her own private, furnished bedroom and bathroom, and it's helpful if the space is somewhat separate from the rest of the family. Live-ins who drive also typically have a car at their disposal, either for transporting the children or for personal use; they also tend to cost more (average $750 a week) because live-ins who drive are the smallest percentage of nannies and thus are in high demand. A lot of parents don't initially like the idea of having someone else living in their home, but live-ins don't necessarily mingle with the family after their hours are done. You will want to map out your rules for privacy at the start so that everybody is comfortable. For example, do you want the nanny to go to her room at a certain time in the evening? Can she have a lock on her door so the children can't go to her when she's off duty? Can the nanny have a friend over or go out at night?

Live-Out

Most nannies are live-out nannies who will commute back and forth to your house each day. At an average rate of $15 per hour, they are more expensive than live-in, and a driving, live-out nanny will command $18 to $20 per hour or more. In general, live-out nannies will have less flexibility in terms of hours and schedules; they will expect to arrive at a certain time, work a set number of hours, and then leave at an agreed-on time as well.

There are some live-out nannies who occasionally live-in—for example, if the parents go away for a week, the nanny may come to stay with the kids, or if the family goes away for the summer, the nanny may live-in at the family's vacation home for those few months. But this is something that needs to be discussed and agreed to by the nanny *before* you hire her. You should not assume that a live-out

---

THE KEY TO A SUCCESSFUL LIVE-IN ARRANGEMENT: PERSONALITY

Whether she's going to be living in for a year or a month, a live-in nanny has to, by nature, be *extremely* adaptable and flexible. Live-in nannies don't have much freedom, and they can get antsy because they're stuck in the job for five straight days. A mellower, more accepting nanny will be fine with this, but a nanny with a stronger personality, who is used to working nine to five and likes plenty of autonomy, will have a harder time. I'm always wary when I interview a nanny who says, "I can do live-in; I've done live-out for twenty years," because, more often than not, nannies who try to make the switch end up feeling suffocated and quitting because it's such a big change.

nanny is willing or able to do live-in, and I have seen many nanny–family relationships severed because the nanny felt that the pressure of being with the family 24/7—even in a beautiful apartment in Rome—was just too much.

Which Arrangement Is Best for You?

If you are still on the fence and have the option of doing either live-in or live-out, it really comes down to your needs as parents regarding those early-morning and after-work hours. If you both work sixty hours a week and travel extensively for your jobs, a live-out situation is very hard to make work. You can do it, but you may end up paying so much for extra, add-on hours and spending so much time arranging backup that it becomes a challenge financially and logistically. With a live-in, you're saving money and you've got the coverage—anything can pop up, any situation can arise, and you're not scrambling.

THE KEY TO A SUCCESSFUL LIVE-OUT ARRANGEMENT: RELIABILITY

I always tell my clients that live-out works best for families with at least one parent who has a fairly predictable schedule. If you both get held up regularly at the office, have commitments after work, or need to travel for business at a moment's notice, you will need to make sure that your live-out nanny has the capacity and desire to cover you during those times. Live-outs themselves also have to be extremely responsible and reliable because they are susceptible to commuting problems due to weather and traffic, so you should factor this into your agreed-on start time and may want to have a backup in the wings just in case.

URBAN VS. SUBURBAN

The second thing to be aware of when hiring a nanny is how your location will affect the parameters of the job. Just as there are major lifestyle differences between the city and the suburbs, urban and suburban nannies often have a different mix of responsibilities. Let's take a look at the differences between urban and suburban nannies, and at how your location should help define your vision for the person you want to hire.

Urban

Being a nanny in the city or a highly walkable urban area is in some ways an easier job because it typically requires less complex navigation. A city nanny may simply come to the family's apartment, feed and dress the child, then walk the stroller three blocks to the playground where the child can socialize with other children. She may run local errands but often she will need to only open the door for dry cleaning and grocery deliveries. If the family lives in an apartment, there is usually a superintendent to call if there's a problem, and if there are other children in the building, the nanny has a ready supply of built-in playdates. The urban nanny can also be less creative with the children because cities tend to have endless options for fun and developmental stimulation. Logistics are straightforward, and everything is usually in close proximity, so it is very easy for her to entertain the children and follow the prescribed order of the day. However, urban nannies need to be savvy enough to handle the hustle and bustle of city life. They need the "street smarts" to keep your child safe at all times, and to deal effectively with crowds, strangers, and the commotion of public transportation.

Suburban

In the suburbs, where the parameters are much looser, nannies need to be much more proactive. If they are driving, suburban nannies will need to be comfortable navigating a potentially unfamiliar town and its surrounding areas as well as driving children to school and activi-

---

NANNY MOBILITY
(AND THE PLIGHT OF THE "SUBURBOUND" NANNY)

As you think about whether you are urban or suburban, bear in mind that mobility plays a big part in any nanny's caregiving abilities. Almost all nannies are happier and will do a better job if they are not tethered to the house. Caring for children is a tiring, all-consuming job, and to give their best, nannies need to be able to step away, get a change of scenery, and recharge. In a city, this is easy to do, but in the suburbs, it is much harder, especially if the nanny doesn't drive. I call these suburban, nondriving nannies "suburbound" nannies because they are limited to the house and immediate neighborhood, and this can be a huge challenge. It may also affect your child's development, because it can be hard for a nanny to keep your child physically and cognitively stimulated when she is bound to the house for long stretches of the day. If you live in the suburbs but cannot afford a driving nanny, you will need to find ways to provide your child with activities and socialization. You can arm your nanny with a variety of toys and crafts. I have also seen suburbound nannies use public transportation, carpools, and even cabs arranged by the parents to attend playdates and classes. If these things are not an option, daycare or preschool may be a better choice.

ties and picking up supplies and groceries on their own. There may or may not be kids in the immediate neighborhood, so they will also need to be comfortable approaching other moms and nannies to set up playdates and be creative enough to come up with things to do if they get stuck in the house on a rainy day. If both parents work full-time, the nanny will need to manage the house and be able to pick up the phone and call the plumber if there's an emergency, so strong language skills are a necessity. In general, suburban nannies need to be equipped to handle a much greater range of everyday duties and concerns.

What Exactly Are a Nanny's Responsibilities?

One of the questions I get asked most frequently by new parents is, "What exactly does a nanny do?" The truth is that while there are a few general parameters, every family's situation is unique, and if you start comparing job descriptions among nannies, it can begin to seem like a nanny can and should do almost anything.

In my experience, when it comes to job duties and responsibilities, there are three main types of nannies: the parental unit nanny, the partner nanny, and the executor nanny. Each of these types is distinguished by their level of autonomy and their ability to handle—or not handle—different types of responsibilities. It's important to know which one you are looking to hire from the get-go because all too often, parents make the mistake of hiring one kind when they really need one of the others. The following descriptions will help you think about your own particular nanny position, the kind of help you need, and identify which of the three nanny types will be best for you.

PARENTAL UNIT NANNY

If your household has two full-time working parents, especially if both parents have inflexible schedules or are a commute away, you *must* have a parental unit nanny. Parental unit nannies can function exactly like a parent, meaning that they are capable of handling every single aspect of the day without any help from Mom or Dad. They can set up playdates, take a child to the doctor, they can do a run to the grocery store, and if your child's school calls with a question, they can answer it. In the suburbs, parental unit nannies drive. They are proactive, self-directed, and comfortable being in charge. They work best with parents who are looking for someone to take the lead in their absence, run the home, and "just take care of it"—whether *it* means mapping out meals for the week, organizing the kids' closets, or running the spelling words every night. Parental unit nannies make it very easy for the parents to transition from work mode to family mode and vice versa because the parents know that everything on the home front is being handled in their absence and done the way they want it.

PARTNER NANNY

The partner nanny is named for her ability to work alongside the mom or primary caregiver and to shift her duties according to the needs of the mother. Partner nannies work well when there is a parent at home or at home part-time. When Mom is out, the partner nanny is able to keep everything related to the children and household running smoothly, and when Mom is at home, the partner nanny works alongside her tackling whatever needs to be done. In the morning, a partner nanny may take the older children to school, run to the store for new ballet shoes, take the baby to music class, and then in the afternoon when Mom comes home, shift her focus to laundry, cooking, or cleaning.

Being a partner nanny is challenging, because it can be difficult to switch back and forth between being the boss and just the helper, so partner nannies need to be highly adaptable and very attuned to the needs of the parent. They also tend to be a different personality type: You can have a partner nanny who is sweet and gentle and a bit more passive; she does not necessarily need to have the parental unit nanny's taste for independence, energy, and drive.

EXECUTOR NANNY

The executor nanny simply carries out the parent's instructions. These nannies work for moms who are at home or at home part-time, and have children who are older and more independent, and they typically do a lot of cleaning and meal preparation, along with small amounts of directed childcare, usually while the mother is there. An executor nanny is not going to be able to take your child on a playdate or do the preschool dropoff, or help you manage your kids' schedules. She may make dinner, but she won't know how to meal plan. Her mind-set is to assist with and execute the tasks assigned to her, and rather than being proactive, she will wait for your direction. Executor nannies are often live-in, so are less expensive, and they can be the perfect solution for moms at home who still want to be the primary caregiver but suddenly find themselves with newborn twins or three kids under the age of five and need an extra set of hands.

Each of these three types of nannies will be capable of handling a wide range of responsibilities, and it will be up to you to decide what those responsibilities are (we'll talk more about this in Chapter 4).

However, there are limits to what you can and should ask your nanny to do. The following section provides some guidelines to help you understand what you have a right to expect—and what you should *not* expect—from your nanny.

What Should You Expect from a Nanny?

In my work with clients, I encounter two extremes in parents. The first are the parents who tiptoe around the nanny and are afraid to ask her to do things—even though she is their employee and it's her job. These are usually the first-time parents, like Alicia and John, who didn't grow up with a nanny and are hesitant about their role as employers. Even if they manage an entire team at work, the personal–professional nature of the nanny relationship throws them, and they end up deferring to the nanny rather than directing her. Or they may be sensitive to cultural or class differences and feel uncomfortable asserting their authority. I meet parents all the time who are fearful of the nanny and refuse to hold her accountable, despite the fact that they are paying her and not getting what they need.

At the other end of the spectrum are the parents who ask too much of the nanny and don't understand why their expectations are inappropriate. These are the parents who expect their nanny to be up all night with a baby, chase after two older children during the day, cook all the meals from scratch, and scrub the toilets in her spare time—all for $500 a week. To them a nanny is not a person, she's a machine.

Your goal as a successful nanny employer is to find the middle ground. As the employer, you are in charge, and your nanny is obligated to respect your wishes and fulfill the duties and responsibilities that you outlined when you hired her. But on the flip side, your nanny is more than just a household employee, like the cleaning lady or the dog walker—she is the person devoting herself to loving, teaching, and caring for your precious little one, and there is no job in the world that's more important. Your expectations for your nanny should be centered not only around the tasks that she performs but also around *the manner in which* she cares for your child. The following lists will help you to gain a deeper understanding of what a nanny is and what you can and should expect your nanny to be—and not to be.

YOUR NANNY IS . . .

A Professional

Being a nanny is a job—a *real* job—just like any other. For many nannies it is their life's work and chosen career, and they take great pride in their ability to do it well. While it may not require a PhD, any seasoned parent knows that there is no substitute for experience when it comes to raising children. The ability to love and nurture a child is not something that can be learned in a classroom, but it does require knowledge, skill, and a tremendous amount of hard work.

Nannies are service professionals who—just like doctors or lawyers—know their worth and want to be compensated fairly for the work they do as well as be respected by their employer for what they bring to the table. They have a right to ask for whatever salary they need, given their experience and the job, as well as to make requests, voice their opinions, and draw the line if they are being treated unkindly or asked to do something unreasonable or unsafe. Unfortunately, nannies often don't get the respect that they deserve. There are plenty of parents (such as those depicted in the bestselling novel *The Nanny Diaries*) who view their nannies as the lowest member of their household and treat them accordingly. I've also seen countless, otherwise normal parents become offended and accuse the nanny of being greedy when she asks for a higher salary than they were hoping to pay or if she asks for a raise when her job parameters change—for example, when the family adds a second child.

I always tell my clients that a big part of a successful nanny–parent relationship is the ability to see things through your nanny's eyes. Even if you come from entirely different backgrounds, you need to remember that your nanny is a professional and to afford her the same consideration and respect that you would expect to get from your own boss. The better you treat your nanny, the more she will give back to your child.

A Caregiver

Good nannies do the job because they truly love children, so in most cases, you should assume that your nanny's primary focus will be your child. From a practical standpoint, this means that she should manage anything that has to do with your child and his or her daily needs. With an infant, the nanny will do feedings, sing songs, play, and put the child down for naps, as well as do light, baby-related housekeeping (such as doing and folding the child's laundry or sterilizing bottles) while the baby sleeps. With toddlers and older children, her duties will expand to include outings, playdates, meal preparation, school transportation, sports and other activities, and homework. Her job is to care for the child and meet his needs whenever the parents aren't around.

But caregiving, in the truest sense of the word, is about far more than just a nanny's physical duties and responsibilities. Being a good caregiver also means caring for a child's *emotional* needs—that is, nurturing the child through positive, loving interactions and relating to him or her in a warm and affectionate way. Many parents tend to think that a nanny is adequate as long as their child is fed and safe, but if the emotional piece of the care is missing, your child won't be getting what he needs. And a lousy nanny can have an impact: Children learn through every exchange with their caregivers, including nonverbal exchanges like cuddling and rocking and having someone smile or laugh back at them. These simple exchanges, so seemingly innocuous to us, actually stimulate key centers in the child's brain and light them up with joy. Studies have shown that children who lack these types of caregiver interaction have smaller brains and fewer neuronal pathways for learning.*

Your nanny's daily interactions with your child, therefore, will lay the foundation for other emotional and social bonds throughout his life. If she is continuously responsive and loving to him, if there is snuggling and playing and laughing throughout the day, if she talks to him with interest and comforts him when he's sad, then your child will feel cherished and secure, and he will thrive. But if a nanny is disengaged, if she stares off into space while feeding the child rather than having a conversation, if she's too tired to listen to the toddler chattering about his day and has zero facial expression (what we call in therapy "flat affect"), it's like putting the child in a darkened room. There are nannies out there who work merely to get the job done; they change the diapers and do the bath, but they don't connect with the child.

Good nannies put the "care" in caregiving by nurturing the whole child—mind, body, and spirit—not just tending to his basic needs. Good nannies may not realize that they are stimulating a child emotionally and socially by reading books, playing games, and talking endlessly to your child throughout the day, but they are. You want to look for someone who is selfless and loving, generous with her affections, and eager to engage and play. You will also want to pay close

* Center on the Developing Child at Harvard University. (2012). "The Science of Neglect: The Persistent Absence of Responsive Care Disrupts the Developing Brain," Working Paper 12, developingchild.harvard.edu.

attention to how the nanny interacts with your child, during in-home trials and after you hire her. If the crucial, emotional piece of the caregiving isn't there—no matter how efficient she is or how flexible or how inexpensive—the nanny is not fit for the job.

A Teacher

Childhood is an amazing journey, filled with great leaps and important milestones. In the first few years of your child's life alone, he will be learning to walk, talk, feed himself, dress himself, use the potty independently, make friends, learn letters and numbers, play games, climb a jungle gym, and understand basic safety rules (such as holding a grown-up's hand while crossing the street). As he gets older, he will begin to tackle bigger things, such as learning responsibility (for example, making his own bed), getting along with others and navigating different social situations, managing schoolwork, and perhaps becoming a big brother. At every stage, he will look to those who are closest to him to guide him—and while that will certainly be you, it will be your nanny too.

The truth is that, depending on the hours that you work, your nanny may very well be present for many or even most of your child's teachable moments, big accomplishments, and firsts. And even if she isn't actually there when your one-year-old says his first word or finally fits the octagon into the shape sorter, she will have been there for all the previous attempts, laying the foundation for his success and guiding him along the way. For babies, toddlers, and even young children, every single day is packed with learning moments, and your nanny will be on deck to demonstrate, explain, answer endless questions, provide encouragement, and cheer wildly when your little one does something great—even if the great achievement is getting Cheerios into his mouth.

Good nannies don't just change diapers and push strollers, they teach our children every single day. Children's brains develop at a remarkably rapid rate, especially during the first three years, and it is the caregiver's job to actively foster cognitive and educational growth. A 2008 study showed that children who are ignored when they begin to babble do not develop language skills at the normal rate, and other studies have shown that activities like play stimulate brain cell activity and can actually increase your child's IQ.*

> Nannies do more to shape the minds and hearts of the children in their care than most people give them credit for.

So in your search, you want to look for candidates who not only are affectionate and reliable but also have the eagerness and ability to engage, encourage, and instruct your child in a positive way. I always tell my clients that they should give their nannies just as much respect as they would a teacher at their child's school. Nannies do more to shape the minds and hearts of the children in their care than most people give them credit for.

A Role Model

In addition to teaching finger feeding and ABCs, good nannies also nurture the children they care for by modeling positive emotional and social behaviors, such as kindness, love, patience, enthusiasm, and polite, appropriate interactions with others. All children learn by watching, listening, imitating, and taking cues from their primary caregivers, so if you have even a part-time nanny, she will, without

---

* Center on the Developing Child at Harvard University. (2012). "The Science of Neglect: The Persistent Absence of Responsive Care Disrupts the Developing Brain," Working Paper 12, developingchild.harvard.edu.

question, be one of your child's most important role models. If your nanny is impatient or her manner is rough or gruff, your child will almost certainly model this behavior. Similarly, if a nanny is timid or anxious because the parents are hyper-demanding and criticize her all the time, the child may also become anxious and fearful. In my practice, I've seen many cases where children cared for by more timid, subservient nannies also display more timid, submissive behavior—and it makes sense. Your nanny is present as an example for your child every single day, so you need to make sure that her example is one you would want your child to follow.

Some parents get very hung up on more superficial things about the nanny that they *don't* want their children to emulate, such as speaking with an accent or dressing a certain way. But in all my experience, I have never once encountered a child who started dressing like the nanny or wound up speaking with an accent because that's what the nanny did. Children don't pay attention to those things, but they are hardwired from birth to model social interactions and behavior. Finding a nanny who can be a role model in terms of her character, demeanor, and approach to life is far more important than finding one who dresses just like you.

WHAT YOU HAVE A RIGHT TO EXPECT FROM A NANNY

- That she is happy, warm, and loving every day
- That she is engaged and interested in your child
- That she is devoted to selflessly caring for all of your child's physical, emotional, and social needs
- That she respect your wishes and rules
- That she behave professionally while on the job and not bring negative energy to work

YOUR NANNY IS NOT . . .
A Maid

If your nanny is already doing your children's laundry and dishes and tidying up their rooms, playroom, and kitchen every day, it can be tempting to ask her to do more. However, if the nanny is home alone and the adult responsible for caring for your child, heavy cleaning—scrubbing bathrooms, washing windows, vacuuming the entire house daily—should not be her responsibility. If you are looking for someone to keep your home spotless, you should hire a housekeeper. Don't put it all on your child's nanny, unless you are at home a great deal to watch the children while she is cleaning.

As any stay-at-home parent will tell you, caring for a child (or children) all day long is *more* than a full-time job. It takes an incredible amount of energy, patience, and creativity to keep children engaged, fed, happy, and out of trouble from the time they get up in the morning until they go to sleep at night. If a nanny is struggling to balance caring for your child with an overly ambitious list of chores, not only will it be very taxing for her but her attention will be divided, and your child will get the short end of the stick. You don't want your nanny to have to pull your toddler away from the playground because she has to go home and finish mopping the floors or be distracted while reading stories because it's Thursday and she's supposed to clean the upstairs bathrooms.

The exceptions to this rule are partner and executor nannies who work with parents who are at home, or at home part-time, and do only limited amounts of hands-on childcare, or nannies who are in charge of school-age children who are more self-sufficient and gone all day. In these scenarios, it may be fine for a nanny to take on additional cleaning around the house, assuming that she's willing to do so.

A Personal Chef

Just as you never want to overload a nanny whose primary focus should be childcare with too much housework, a nanny who is by herself caring for young children round-the-clock will have minimal time to prepare extensive meals. If you are looking for someone to create complex meal plans for the entire family, shop for food, chop and prep ingredients, and have an elaborate dinner ready for everyone when you get home from work, you need a cook, not a nanny.

I once worked with a family who had three young boys all under the age of five. The parents were at their wit's end because their nannies kept quitting and they couldn't figure out why. When I dug deeper, I learned that the boys were extremely rowdy, that the parents wanted the nanny to prepare fresh-cooked, extremely complex organic dishes for the entire family, *and* that they had a rule about no iPads or TV. I asked them how on earth they expected the nanny to be able to go out daily to find the freshest fish and protein, chop and prepare ingredients, cook them, and get dinner on the table, all while keeping an eye on three very young boys—when she couldn't even use television or electronics to get them to sit still for a half hour!

Parents may think that nannies are miracle workers, but preparing meals takes time and focus and is especially challenging if the nanny is caring for infants and small children. Plus there are safety issues: Hot pots and burners, open flames, and knives can all lead to trouble if a nanny is distracted. Unless there is a parent at home to manage the children, the children nap a great deal, or the children are old enough to keep an eye on themselves safely, your nanny should be allowed to focus on feeding your children rather than on being the family's personal chef.

Common Myths That Parents Have About Nannies

While many parents come to the nanny experience without a full understanding of a nanny's role and responsibilities, I have also found that there are certain myths about nannies that persist among parents—even those who strive to be well informed. These mistaken beliefs prevent good decision making during the search and almost always lead to trouble after a nanny is hired. Whenever I sit down with a new set of parents, I like to start off by setting the record straight so that they can approach their situation in the right frame of mind, with realistic expectations.

MYTH 1: HIRING A NANNY IS THE SAME AS HIRING A BABYSITTER

It's not. Babysitters are present only in short fits and spurts—they don't have to be great, they just have to be competent. But a nanny is someone who will be there *every* day and play a key role in your child's development. I've had parents say, "I just need to get a warm body in here," but parenting doesn't stop when you're not present, so you want to provide your children with the single best tutor, coach, counselor, and teacher possible to represent your values and wishes when you're not there. In addition, the nanny–parent relationship is one of the most complex, multifaceted ones on the planet (more about this in Chapter 11). This is someone who will be intimately involved with your family and may know more about your personal life than some of your closest friends. You want to take a lot of time and care with this decision because the nanny will become another member of your family, and the product of her work is a living, growing child.

MYTH 2: A GOOD NANNY WILL BE ABLE TO COME IN AND AUTOMATICALLY KNOW HOW TO CARE FOR YOUR CHILD

Wrong. You will never be able to find someone who cares for your child perfectly from day one, no matter how much experience she has. Even if someone has been a nanny for thirty years, she has never been a nanny in *your* home before. Every set of parents and every child is different, so training—the more extensive, the better—is a must with any nanny you hire. Unless you give specific, thorough directions about how you want things done, the nanny will come in and do things *her* way, which may or may not work for you and your child. Even if you are looking for someone to run the show (and many full-time working parents are), you still need to provide the nanny with a detailed overview of your children, your household, your preferences, and your rules.

More than half of the problems that arise between nannies and parents occur because the parents have failed to give the nanny proper guidance and instruction. Fortunately, this also means that many nanny issues can be remedied simply through adequate training— and it's never too late. We'll talk more about how to use training to improve the performance of an existing nanny in Part 3.

MYTH 3: IT'S EASIER TO CARE FOR OTHER PEOPLE'S CHILDREN THAN FOR YOUR OWN

Wrong. It's harder. With your own children, you can bend the rules and change them as you go. You can let your child sleep in the car seat in the garage or leave her crying while you take two minutes to brush your teeth. Nannies can't. You can take a day off and park your child in front of the TV or be grumpy before you've had your coffee or lose your temper when your child colors on the dog with indelible marker or decides to cut her own hair. Nannies can't. In fact, being a nanny is basically every bit as challenging and exhausting and constant as being a parent but without any of the leeway that, as parents, we give ourselves from time to time.

One of the biggest things I try to impress on parents is that being a nanny is a hard job. You have to be many different things to different people: You have to be a mother but also a helper; you have to be proactive but also deferential; you have to make it personal by giving your affection and care to the child but keep it professional with the parents. Many nannies work twelve-hour days and commute for an hour or more to get to and from their jobs. They may be leaving their own children so that they can earn a living, and many nannies have left their entire families behind to come to the United States in search of a better life. When the toddler is on her tenth tantrum of the day, and the preteen is sassing back, and the five-year-old tips over the entire gallon of orange juice onto the floor, a mother has her love for her children to pull her through. But a nanny has to rely on her own reserves of patience, strength, and determination to help her persevere.

> Being a nanny is a hard job.

The fact that a nanny is a professional doesn't make the realities of the job any easier, so you need to afford her the utmost respect. Nothing requires more time, energy, and personal discipline than being a good parent—except trying to parent someone else's kid.

MYTH 4: IF WE'RE PAYING HER, SHE SHOULD DO WHATEVER WE ASK

Some parents think that just because they're paying a nanny's salary, they are entitled to ask the world of her well beyond caregiving. I've had parents who are running their nanny ragged say to me, "I don't care if she's tired, I'm paying her to watch these kids!" But taking advantage of your nanny is not only wrong, it can lead to safety issues. Nobody can be up all night with a baby and then chase after two older children all day long without mistakes and accidents occurring. If you stretch your nanny to her limit and assign her more work than she can possibly handle, your children will suffer, she is going to end up quitting, and no one wins.

There is an illusion among some parents that money can buy you anything. It can't. Just because you are paying someone to do a job doesn't make it right. As I said earlier, there are some things that parents have a right to expect from a nanny: that she be warm and loving, that she respect your rules, and that she be devoted to caring for all of your child's physical and emotional needs. But unless you discuss it ahead of time and the nanny agrees, you do not have a right to ask your nanny to do anything that is not immediately related to your child, such as assuming she will do housekeeping or cooking for the entire family, no matter how much you pay. Some younger or inexperienced nannies, especially those who are new to the country, may desperately need the money and be uncomfortable saying no to an employer, especially if their legal status is in question. This is when exploitation occurs, and it's up to parents everywhere to draw the line.

I always remind my clients: *If your nanny is exhausted and overburdened, she is not going to be at her best for your child.* Accidents happen when people are tired and distracted, and you want her to bring her A-game every single day. Above all, you need to be realistic about your expectations and recognize that your nanny is a person, just like you.

MYTH 5: YOUR NANNY IS LUCKY
TO HAVE THIS JOB

Yes, there are a lot of nannies out there, and yes, it's a bad economy. But you can never appreciate a good nanny too much, and you can never say thank you enough. In my experience, too many parents have a backward notion of gratitude when it comes to nannies. They feel like the nanny should be grateful to *them*, instead of the other way around.

> You can never appreciate a good nanny too much, and you can never say thank you enough.

I once had a client who had a live-out nanny who changed to live-in for the summer. The family had a house in the Hamptons, and once the two older children were out of school, they packed up the entire household and moved to the beach. The nanny, however, felt angry and resentful because even though her workload had tripled—she was now in charge of watching three children all day long instead of a single toddler, and her hours extended well into the night—the family had flatly refused to pay her any additional money.

When I explained the nanny's position to the mom, she looked at me like I had two heads. "Tammy," she responded, "she's getting a summer at the beach! Her room is enormous with luxury-brand linens, the house has gorgeous views of the ocean, she's at the beach all day with the kids, and she gets organic food at every meal!"

"Allison," I fired back, "she's the *nanny*! She's not vacationing in the Hamptons for the summer. This isn't fun for her. It's her job!"

Almost every set of parents I meet thinks that they are the best, most reasonable employers and that their kids are the best, most charming kids—even when the evidence suggests otherwise. And many parents feel that any nanny who works for them should thank their lucky stars to be getting a share of their hard-earned cash each week. But this attitude is arrogant and misguided. While it is true that there are a lot of available nannies, *good* nannies are always in high demand and will have their choice of who they work for. Yes, you can always find another one, but she may not be the *right* one. This is why, if you have a good nanny, you want to treat her extremely well and do whatever you can to keep her.

And remember, even if you think that your kids are wonderful and that you are the easiest, best employers in the world, if this person is caring for your child, *you* are lucky to have *her*.

No nanny is perfect, but when you hire a nanny with your eyes wide open and a true sense of the job and what to expect, you stand the best chance possible of finding the right person and building a relationship that lasts. In Part 2, we'll look at the Gold Standard hiring process and how it can lead you to a great match.

WHAT YOU DO *NOT* HAVE A RIGHT TO EXPECT FROM YOUR NANNY

- That she do housework above and beyond that which is related to your child, or prepare meals for the entire family (unless your circumstances allow for it, and your nanny has agreed to it at the beginning)
- That she be able to do the job without any specific training
- That she work past her regular hours without pay (unless agreed to previously)
- That she take on additional duties beyond those specified in your original agreement

PART TWO

The Gold Standard
Hiring Process

CHAPTER 3

———•———

Who Are You?

Doing a Family Needs Assessment

If you're looking to hire a new nanny, this chapter marks the start of your journey to finding am amazing caregiver for your child. The Gold Standard hiring process is all about matching your and your child's needs to the personal and professional qualities of the nanny, so I always tell parents that they have to look at themselves first before they can look for someone to hire. Before you go any further, this chapter is designed to help you answer these questions: Who are you? What do you want in a nanny? And what type of scenario is going to work best for your family?

Most parents who set out to hire a nanny approach the process backward: They round up a random assortment of candidates referred to them by friends and friends of friends, interview the nannies *first*, decide which ones they like, and then try to figure out who can match their actual logistical needs. But unless you figure out your exact job criteria at the outset, you will spend a lot of time and energy meeting with candidates who ultimately, for one reason or other, aren't right for the job. Working and at-home parents are extremely busy, and no one wants to waste extra time on the nanny search process. But if you try to rush things, no matter how many great candidates you see, you are not going to have sufficient information to make the smartest, best choice.

Whenever I start a new nanny search for a client, I always sit down with the parents to discuss their wishes and feelings about nannies in great detail. I ask them not only about the salary and the hours they need but about their general impressions of nannies, good or bad, as well as their parenting style and what type of personality they think they would prefer in a nanny, and why. Suddenly, with a little prompting, all sorts of emotions and preferences come up: They may not want a Spanish-speaking nanny because they had a bad experience with a Spanish-speaking nanny as a child, or they don't want someone who smacks her chewing gum, or they prefer a calm, serene home environment and don't want someone who is loud and boisterous. Some of these preferences may seem nitpicky, but when someone is going to be in your home for thirty, forty, fifty, or even sixty hours a week, any preference—no matter how small—needs to be taken into account.

My Family Needs Assessment (FNA) form (see page 263) is designed to help you clearly identify what you want *and* don't want in a nanny, so that you can easily spot the candidates who have what you need and screen for any potential problems as you go. It also helps you to pinpoint the details and nuances, both positive and negative, of your particular nanny position—details that the nanny *must* be able to handle if she is going to succeed. This form grew out of my work as a therapist and is based on the traditional Biopsychosocial Assessment that therapists give to patients during their initial session. Whereas the typical intake form at a nanny agency will focus only on the physical details of the job, such as the duties and the days, my FNA looks at the emotional piece as well (for example, your personal communication style) along with your child's specific developmental needs. By asking these questions, you will come to better understand yourself as an employer as well as your nanny job and what it requires.

Understanding your job from the beginning is crucial because, as many parents will tell you, trying to add additional responsibilities or change the parameters of the job after your nanny has already started can be tricky. Countless nanny–parent relationships have soured because the parents change the rules of the game or keep asking the nanny for more and more help with duties that don't necessarily involve the children. I was once called in to do mediation between a mom and nanny who were completely at odds because the family had gone out and gotten a puppy and expected the nanny to take care of it during the day. The nanny felt that she was a

> You can't change the requirements of the job once a nanny's in it.

childcare professional and not a pet sitter or a dog walker, and she was angry that the parents had just assumed that she'd shoulder most of the responsibility.

This is why I always stress to clients that *you can't change the requirements of the job once a nanny's in it.* You may ask for changes, but you have no right to expect or demand them if they haven't been agreed on from the start. That's why it's so important to have all your ducks in a row at the *beginning* of the hiring process, because it's likely that you won't be able to go back and change things once you're done. It is far better to present your worst-case scenario in terms of responsibilities than to hire a nanny for an easier position and then try to add to the job.

How to Approach Your Family Needs Assessment

The key to doing an effective FNA is to take your time and *just be honest*. You should include all the things you like and don't like or want or don't want, no matter how silly or insignificant they may seem. Don't worry about what you think you're supposed to say or feel about nannies or what anybody else will think of your answers— this exercise is for no one's eyes but yours. This is your chance to define your job and create your vision of the perfect nanny. If you've previously worked with nannies or other childcare providers, use your past experiences to guide you.

The form is made up of four different sections: Physical Job Description, Job Duties and Responsibilities, Emotional Job Description, and Summing Up. The rest of this chapter walks you through the entire FNA and provides guidance on how to think about each question and interpret your response. As you complete the FNA, you should write down your answers in a designated "Nanny Search" notebook or type them out on your computer because you will need to be able to refer back to your earlier answers to see the big picture and draw conclusions. By the end of the form, you will have identified the Musts, Pluses, and Deal-Breakers for your job and have determined what your own personal Gold Standard for nannies is going to be. You'll find a blank form on page 263 and can also download forms at tammygold.com.

PART 1: PHYSICAL JOB DESCRIPTION

The Physical Job Description is an overview of the basic parameters of the job: logistical details and criteria that will most likely remain the same no matter who or what type of nanny you hire. If you haven't already done so, this is the time to figure out the days and hours of your job, whether you want live-in or live-out, whether you will need your nanny to drive, and other practical considerations. Many of these decisions, however, are not as straightforward as they seem; there are usually a number of X factors connected to your unique situation that you don't want to overlook. Even if you think you already know the answers to these questions, I encourage you to read the following tips for thinking about each item to make sure that you are approaching each decision with as much awareness and insight as possible:

1. **Days for this position.** When it comes to deciding your days, I always tell people, "Don't make this decision based on what you think a nanny job *should* be." Even if you think that a typical nanny works nine to five, Monday to Friday, you are going to be paying for this care, so you need to get the days that are most beneficial for you and your family. If your schedule follows the standard workweek, fine. But if you want Wednesday to Friday or round-the-clock care seven days a week, then do it. Any scenario is fine as long as you can afford it.

If you're working, you should consider whether you want to have coverage on non-workdays as well. For example, if you work part-time two days a week, but still want some extra coverage so you can run errands, go to the gym, or have one-on-one time with your children individually, you might do four days rather than two. Or maybe you want to build in a half day on Saturday so that you and your partner can have a date night every week. Remember that caring for yourself is important too, so if overlapping with your nanny for an extra day will be extremely helpful and the cost is not an issue, don't be afraid to ask for it.

2. **Hours for each day.** As with days, you want to make sure you get the hours that are most beneficial for you. Often parents say nine to

five when they really need seven to seven, so I always tell people that it's better to add more hours at first so you make sure you get what you need, and your candidates get a true sense of the scope of the job. Many parents, understandably, don't want to pay for more hours than are absolutely necessary, so they try to economize and do the "hand-off"—when mom comes home and the nanny is out the door. But I can tell you that this is harder than it seems and that most parents (and kids) really do need some extra time when both they and the nanny are there together so that they can transition smoothly and exchange information about the day. Unless you are completely in charge of your own hours, *don't* make the mistake of erring on the side of optimism. It is much smarter to add in an extra hour or two from the beginning so that you make sure you find a nanny who is fine with staying late if need be, and you avoid having to pay lots of additional overtime.

3. Preferred start date. When you think about your start date, try to allow some amount of time for you to be at home with the nanny after she starts—even if it's just a few days. As I will discuss in more detail, training is essential for every nanny, and this way you can be on hand to give instructions and answer questions as she adjusts to your household and routine. Knowing your start date will also help you decide whether to consider candidates who are currently working for other families and may need to give two or more weeks' notice before they start.

4. Where do you need your nanny to live? This question is all about deciding whether you need your nanny to live-in, live-out, or do a combination of both. You should refer to the overviews of live-in and live-out nannies in Chapter 2 and decide which scenario will work best for your family given your living situation and the days, hours, and type of coverage that you need. If you're planning to do a combination of both, you should pinpoint the exact circumstances in which your nanny will become live-in (for example, during family vacations or while you are traveling for work).

5. If this is a live-out position. This series of questions asks you to think about the logistics of a live-out situation, and how far away the nanny can live and still meet your needs. If you live in an area with readily accessible public transportation, commuting isn't usually a problem. But if you live in the suburbs and aren't within walking distance of a train station or bus stop, you need to figure out how your nanny will get to work. You will also need to decide how much distance is too much: If she lives two hours away and you work long hours or you think there may be situations or emergencies where you'd like her to be available, a two-hour commute isn't going to work.

You will also need to decide if you are willing to cover any of the cost of the transportation for her commute, should she request it. New York City nannies, for example, expect all of their transportation costs to be covered, so the majority of New York parents provide their nanny with a monthly pass for public transit. Similarly, suburban nannies who drive to work may get reimbursed for some of the mileage and gas. Parents will also typically provide their nannies with money for a cab or car service home if she has to work later than usual and travel late at night. You will need to do your research and figure out what a nanny in your area will expect and what the exact parameters will be (for example, after what time will you provide money for a taxi home?). If you truly cannot afford this type of compensation, you will need to have an honest discussion with your candidates, explain why you can't do it, and tell them that you hope to be able to do it down the line.

> Our nanny suggested that we share a monthly subway pass during her interview, which I thought was a great idea. It works perfectly: She uses the pass to come to work, hands it to me, and then I use it to get to work and hand it back to her when I get home.
>
> —ALEXIS, NEW YORK, NY

The final question that you'll want to consider with a live-out nanny is whether there will be times when you want her to live-in. Now is the time to think about those scenarios so you can broach them with candidates during the screening process and make sure that they are willing to do this. Most nannies are happy to stay overnight on occasion, as long as they don't have children of their own, but many live-out nannies may balk at more extended scenarios, such as being at the beach with your family for an entire month. You will also need to decide how the nanny will be compensated when she does live-in: Will she be paid an overtime rate? You want to make sure you're on the same page from the start, so there's no conflict down the road.

6. If this is a live-in position. This series of questions asks you to drill down on the logistics of a live-in nanny situation. For starters, now is the time to figure out what accommodations will be provided for the nanny. Will she have a private bathroom or be required to share with the children? Are there areas of your home that will be off limits to the nanny or off limits after certain hours?

You will also need to think about food, and how and where the nanny will eat. Some live-in nannies will bring food they've cooked from home at the beginning of the week, but it may last through only Wednesday, so for the rest of the week she will need to be able to cook. You will also need to decide if she is going to eat with the children or the rest of the family, or if you would prefer that she eat in her room after a certain time. You should also have a plan for how she will get her food. In a live-out situation, employers are not required to provide food (although most will stock the kitchen with snacks and a few other things that the nanny likes), but in a live-in situation, the employer pays for the nanny's food and often does her shopping for her. She can either eat everything you're eating, which most nannies will do, or you can ask her to give you a list and pick up whatever she needs for the week.

I also tell my clients that, unless you absolutely need 24/7 coverage and are up front about that with your candidates from the beginning, your live-in nanny—just like a live-out nanny—should have a clear start time in the morning and a time when she goes off duty at night. Nannies also need time to themselves, and they need to know that after 8 p.m. (for example), they can retire to their room and relax. If she is required to assist with the children during the night or on weekends, you will need to discuss that up front. Some live-in nannies have no problem helping out during the night for no extra charge, and some will want to be compensated for that additional time.

7. Do you need your nanny to drive? If you live in an urban area with an extensive public transit system and walkable neighborhood, maybe not. But if you live in the suburbs, a nanny who drives is almost always helpful, even if there is a parent at home. You should also think about under what circumstances your nanny will drive: Will she simply drive as a part of her commute or will she be driving your children to different activities and running errands that require a car?

8. If your nanny will be driving. The next few questions prompt you to think about logistics and possible Musts for your job description that are related to having a driving nanny. For example, will she be using one of your cars or will she have to provide her own? Will she be covered by your auto insurance policy or will she have to supply her own? In addition, if she will be using her own car to shuttle your children around town—rather than just getting to and from work—it is standard for parents to provide either a weekly stipend for gas or reimbursement based on mileage, so you will need to budget for this and factor it into your weekly costs.

Keep in mind that any nanny who is going to be driving on your watch *must* have a valid driver's license, and therefore she will need to be a legal resident or U.S. citizen. This is something that you will need to screen for and confirm as you go through the hiring process.

9. Does your nanny need to know how to swim? If you have a pool or spend summers at the beach, it is highly advisable to have a nanny who swims, especially if she will be supervising the children on her own. In urban areas, finding a nanny who swims can sometimes be a challenge, so I always ask parents if they are willing to pay for their nanny to take swimming lessons. If so, you should broach this with any nonswimming candidates to see if they are open to learning.

10. Would you like your nanny to speak a second language? Parents tend to get crazed about this because they love the idea of their child learning a second language, and it feels like another way to maximize their dollar. But I think that second languages should be viewed as a Plus rather than a Must because requiring someone to speak fluent French or Mandarin Chinese to your child all day long will greatly narrow your list of potential candidates, and might blind you to more important factors like demeanor and personality type. Second-language scenarios usually work best if at least one of the parents is a native speaker rather than relying on a nanny to do double duty as a de facto language coach.

Whenever foreign languages come up, I remind parents that while a good nanny is a teacher in a hundred small ways every day, teaching foreign language skills is not the most important part of her job. Furthermore, as a parent, you always want as much information as possible about what's going on with your nanny in your house, and if there's a language barrier, you won't be getting the full picture. If foreign language exposure is very important to you, it can certainly be one of the factors in your decision—but only if the rest of the match is right.

11. Will your nanny need to be able to travel? Travel is one of the main areas where a nanny's legal status can present a problem. A nanny who is not a U.S. citizen or legal resident or who does not have an appropriate visa will be unable to travel domestically by plane or leave and reenter the country. If you are going to need your nanny to travel, you will need to make sure that she is comfortable with the prospect and can provide documentation that proves she is able to do so.

12. If you said yes to travel. This series of questions asks you to think further about the details of any travel, so that you are prepared to outline your expectations to the nanny. You will need to give her a realistic sense of how frequent the trips will be and how long they are likely to last. You will also need to agree on a travel pay rate. Travel rates will vary, depending on your market and what a nanny received at her previous job, but a flat rate of around $50 extra a day for weekdays and $75 extra a day for weekends are not uncommon.

13. Are there any other benefits or perks you will provide? This is the time to think about any special perks and nonmonetary enhancements you can offer your nanny based on your family's unique work and home situation. These special add-ons can come in extremely

ADDITIONAL LOGISTICS:
THINKING ABOUT SALARY AND BENEFITS

Just as important as figuring out what you need from your nanny is how much you can afford to pay her. Thinking about salary ahead of time is crucial because you don't want to spend time checking references and doing interviews with someone who you ultimately can't afford to hire. I always recommend that my clients do a weekly rate rather than an hourly one because, in general, a weekly rate is less expensive than if you were to calculate the week's salary hour by hour. Nannies generally have a "magic number" in their head that is the amount of money they need to make each week—for example, $700— and once they've met it, they're happy and don't get hung up on the exact hours. What that magic number is will depend on the average rates for your area (you can find this out by asking friends or plugging in your zip code on Care.com), the nanny's previous salary, and the kinds of duties involved in your job. I usually advise parents to come up with two numbers: the first number is what you *want* to pay, and the second is what you would be *willing* to pay if the most amazing nanny ever walked through your door. I recommend a range of $200.

You should also think about any additional compensation and benefits that your nanny will receive so that you are prepared to discuss them during the process and when you make an offer. These include the following:

- **Overtime.** Overtime refers to any hours beyond what you and the nanny agree will be standard for your job. Under the Fair Labor Standards Act, live-out nannies who charge an hourly rate are entitled to an overtime rate of time and a half. If you do a weekly rate, you should expect to pay a little above the average hourly rate for your area. Some nannies will command higher rates for weekends, holidays, and travel.

- **Bonuses.** Most nannies, both full-time and part-time, will expect to receive an annual bonus of one to two weeks' pay.

You should decide now how much you will pay and when you will pay it so that you can present it to the nanny as a part of your offer.

- **Health insurance.** Providing health insurance is not standard, but it may be required for some nannies hired through high-end agencies. Health insurance is expensive, so I usually recommend that parents keep it in their back pocket and use it to sweeten the deal only if the negotiation gets tough. In some cases the family will choose and pay for a new policy; in others they will pay the nanny an annual or monthly stipend to cover all or part of the premium cost of a plan that she selects.

- **Holidays.** Nannies typically get the standard big six: New Year's Day, Memorial Day, Fourth of July, Labor Day, Thanksgiving, and Christmas. Anything in addition to these six will need to be a part of your negotiation. Be sure to discuss exactly which holidays she gets up front so there is no confusion later on.

- **Vacation.** Standard vacation is one to two weeks with pay. Parents usually stipulate that they get to choose one week—often chosen to coincide with a family vacation so they don't need to pay for extra childcare coverage—and the nanny gets to choose the other one. If you have a flexible schedule, you can offer more in exchange for a lower weekly rate or as a perk if the nanny is choosing between offers.

- **Sick days and personal days.** Parents usually group these together and offer three to five per year, to be used as the nanny needs them. When it comes to sick days, however, I recommend a more flexible policy, if you can manage it, because ideally you don't want your nanny coming into work and sharing her illness with everyone else in the house. Instead of a number, you can say "unlimited within reason" or "with approval."

handy when you are negotiating, especially if the nanny is choosing between you and another family. For example, if you work from home, maybe you can offer her half-day Fridays or one Friday off each month with pay. I've also seen parents offer their live-in nanny things like a monthly yoga pass, personal use of the family car, free use of the family accountant when doing taxes, and classes—anything from English as a second language (ESL) to continuing education or CPR.

PART 2: JOB DUTIES AND RESPONSIBILITIES

Now that you've outlined the basics of your nanny position, it's time to put some additional thought into what your nanny will be doing day to day. This section of the FNA starts with the big picture and helps you determine your ideal nanny type, before moving on to help you figure out what your nanny's exact duties are going to be. It's important to be as specific here as possible, so that when it's time for screening and interviews, you are able to give each candidate a crystal-clear picture of what the job entails, and use the Gold Standard process to match your needs—duty by duty—to her qualifications and experience.

1. What type of nanny are you looking for? As discussed in Chapter 2, there are three main types of nannies: the parental unit nanny, the partner nanny, and the executor nanny. For this question, you should refer to the descriptions beginning on page 25 and decide which one most accurately describes your needs and the kind of nanny–parent relationship you are looking for. Once you know your general type, you can use it as a snapshot to quickly assess potential candidates to see if they meet your requirements.

2. What will be your nanny's child-related duties and responsibilities? This question provides you with a list of typical child-related tasks and duties and asks you to select which ones you'd like your nanny to be responsible for. As when choosing your days and hours, *do not* underestimate the amount of help you are going to need, especially if you and your partner both work full-time. Every item on this list is standard and should be completely acceptable to any parental unit or partner nanny, so don't be afraid of checking the tasks that seem more like housekeeping, such as tidying up the child's bedroom or emptying the diaper pail.

☐ Wake children
☐ Prepare bottles
☐ Bottle feedings
☐ Sterilize baby bottles
☐ Wash baby bottles
☐ Wash/sterilize pacifiers
☐ Wash/sterilize toys
☐ Tidy playroom
☐ Pick up toys
☐ Tummy time
☐ Plan meals
☐ Prepare meals
☐ Serve meals
☐ Clean up kitchen after meals
☐ Pack school lunches
☐ Dress children
☐ Wash children's laundry

☐ Fold/put away clothes
☐ Organize closets
☐ Diaper changes
☐ Restock diapers and wipes
☐ Restock diaper bag
☐ Empty diaper pail
☐ Bath
☐ Tidy bathroom after bath
☐ Tidy bedroom
☐ Child-related errands
☐ Doctor's visits
☐ Listen to music
☐ Plan activities/ playdates
☐ Take to activities/ playdates
☐ Indoor play

☐ Outside play
☐ School dropoff
☐ School pickup
☐ Unpack backpacks
☐ Homework
☐ Read
☐ Tutoring
☐ Work with teachers
☐ Work with therapists
☐ Organize sports equipment
☐ Buy gifts for birthday parties
☐ Create a schedule
☐ Maintain specified schedule
☐ Manage calendar
☐ Daily communication log
☐ Bedtime

3. If you have a child with special needs, are there any additional duties or responsibilities that the nanny will have regarding this child? Nannies can be an enormous help to special-needs children and their parents. If you have a child who requires occupational therapy, physical therapy, speech therapy, or sensory training, finding a nanny who is able to assist with these therapies can make a huge amount of difference. However, if the nanny is going to be doing the exercises in your absence and will need to have special training or learn certain techniques, you will need to specify this up front so you can find the right hire. There are plenty of nannies who will be able to assist you or any therapists who come to your house, but not as many who will have the skills or ability to do it on their own. For this reason, nannies who do have training and specialize in caring for special-needs children usually cost more, and they are almost always live-out, part-time, and paid by the hour ($18 to $25 per hour is normal).

4. Are there any other healthcare duties that must be performed for any of your children on a regular schedule? The two biggest healthcare responsibilities that today's nannies face are managing medications and allergies. I've seen a lot of situations where parents put their executor nannies, or nannies with limited reading and language skills, in charge of handling sensitive medications, and it can lead to real trouble. If you have a child with ADD or ADHD who requires very finely tuned morning and evening doses of medication or a child with a life-threatening peanut allergy, you need a highly competent nanny with an extremely discerning eye.

With medications, food allergies, and any other health-related issues, you should ask the nanny about them during the interview, get a sense of her familiarity and comfort level, assess her willingness to learn, and then role-play exactly what you expect her to do during a trial. Competency in these areas is not something you can assess over the phone, but you can definitely test for it live to make sure that she can read and comprehend ingredient labels and medical information. Other issues that require hands-on management may include childhood diabetes, a history of febrile seizures, or asthma.

5. What additional household duties do you wish the nanny to perform? Of all the potential responsibilities that a nanny may have, there is none more varied—and often more contentious—than housekeeping. Some nannies draw a hard line when it comes to housework, while others may prefer it to be the bulk of their job. While I strongly believe that quality care for your child is far more important than having a spotless house and that overburdening or distracting a nanny with too many chores can lead to problems, I also

---

YOUR HOUSEHOLD DUTIES: HOW MUCH IS TOO MUCH?

I always tell parents that when you're thinking about housework, you should look at your child's daily schedule, hour by hour, and *realistically* assess how much time your nanny will have for extra tasks. If you have a baby who naps twice a day for several hours, there is certainly time in the nanny's schedule to do light cleaning and tidying up. Even if you have an active toddler who takes a good nap in the afternoon, there should still be time to do a few select household chores. However, if you have multiple children of different ages, or a child who naps for only forty-five minutes at a time, you need to realize that the nanny will be on her toes all day long and most likely won't have time to multitask. You should never expect your nanny to do anything that you would be unable to do, and you never want her to get to the point where she's thinking, "I really want to read to the baby, but I need to please the parents, and I still have to mop the kitchen and run the vacuum..."

If I had to go back and do it all over again, I would definitely find a nanny who could help us take care of the house. When we were interviewing, we used a list of questions that we got from a popular parenting website and one of them was, "Are you open to doing housework?" And most of the nannies, including the one we hired, said, "No, my focus is the child." We liked that in a way—as parents, that's what you want to hear—but now that we're a year into it, it also means that my house is a mess. The real frustration is when I come home at 6 p.m., and I'm exhausted, and I know that our nanny was sitting around for a lot of the day while our son napped, and there are dishes in the sink, and the floor could use a good sweeping . . . If she has so much extra time, there are plenty of things I could have her doing, but it wasn't a part of our original agreement, so we're stuck.

—MARGOT, SEATTLE, WA

believe that good nannies are there to help the entire family, and that in many situations, it is perfectly reasonable to ask for some additional assistance around the house. The key is to define what you need early on so that it is a nonnegotiable part of your job description from the start. For example, "Our child's care is obviously our top priority, but I'm a working mother and I'm gone fifty hours a week, so I really need someone to make the beds every day, unload the dishwasher, and sweep up after mealtimes."

Some parents are overly cautious about asking for help with housework, but I always tell those parents—especially those who work full-time—to really think hard and be realistic about what they need. The truth is that being a working parent is tough. It's exhausting to put in a full day at the office and then come home and be on for the most challenging part of the day. When you walk through the front door, you are not going to want to walk in and see a sink full of dirty dishes, cat hair all over the couch, and a week's worth of laundry piled up. Because you are creating the job and paying the salary, now is the time to think about what would be most helpful to you, and put those needs on paper so they become one of your Pluses or Musts.

This question provides you with a list of possible household duties and asks you to identify which ones—if any—you'd like your nanny to do. Some of the tasks that involve heavier cleaning (such as bathrooms, windows, and mopping) are really doable only if you have an executor or partner nanny who isn't devoting most of her time to childcare. You should go through the list, check which ones you want, and write down any additional duties that are specific to your home. If you already have a housekeeper, you may not need any additional help from your nanny at all.

☐ Family laundry
☐ Fold and put away clothes
☐ Family dishes
☐ Make all beds
☐ Change sheets
☐ Tidy main living areas
☐ Windows
☐ Bathrooms
☐ Vacuuming
☐ Mopping
☐ Sweeping
☐ Empty wastebaskets
☐ Dust
☐ Maintain grocery list
☐ Grocery shopping
☐ Bring in mail

☐ Bring in newspaper
☐ Take out trash
☐ Take out recycling
☐ Wipe down counters
☐ Clean out refrigerator
☐ Organize pantry
☐ Organize all closets
☐ Organize entry areas
☐ Organize mail
☐ Run errands
☐ Dry cleaning
☐ Be at home to meet and manage housekeeper, plumber, electrician, etc.
☐ If live-in, clean and maintain own living area

6. If the nanny is required to cook, what will her specific cooking duties be? This question asks you to think further about any cooking that you want your nanny to do. You will first need to figure out what *cooking* means for you: Does it mean preparing fresh meals for the entire family from start to finish? Does it mean cooking easy dishes for the kids only, like grilled cheese and scrambled eggs? Or does it mean prepping so you can do the cooking when you get home, or partnering with you each day to help get dinner on the table?

There are many nannies who are happy to cook, but as discussed in Chapter 2, cooking can also become a problem if the nanny is being asked to prepare labor-intensive meals and care for very young children at the same time. My overall feeling and advice to clients is that serious cooking is best left to partner and executor nannies who have a mom around to help them or parental unit nannies who are caring for older, more independent children.

7. Do you observe any religious dietary laws or have any dietary restrictions/preferences that the nanny must follow while in your home? If you keep kosher or are vegetarian, or if someone in your home has a particular food allergy, you will need to be clear about any specific guidelines that you want the nanny to follow while she's in your house. One way to simplify things is to have the nanny prepare, cook, and eat only food that you provide. But if you don't want the added expense of feeding your nanny, you will need to present your candidates with a reasonable set of rules from the get-go so you can be sure that they are willing to comply.

A lot of parents who follow a certain dietary regimen such as vegan or macrobiotic for lifestyle reasons get very hung up on finding a nanny who eats the same way. But my feeling is that as long as someone is willing to observe your rules while in your home, how they eat on their own time doesn't really matter. Listing a particular way of eating as a Must for your job—rather than just a Plus—will constrain your search a great deal and cause you to overlook candidates who may be a fit in more important ways.

8. If driving is involved in the job, what are the driving duties required? Because you've already given some thought to driving in the Physical Job Description section, you probably have a good idea of when, and under what circumstances, your nanny will be required to drive. This question asks you to pinpoint the exact driving duties and frequency, so that you can give your candidates the most accurate picture possible. Whether you need only the occasional errand, or school dropoff and pickup every single day, the nanny needs to know.

9. If there are pets in your home, will the nanny be required to care for them? Issues around pets can be a very big deal, and there is no end to the strife that they cause between parents and nannies. For this reason, it is essential that you be frank about any pets and pet-related duties at the start of your hiring process. Some nannies are allergic to cats and dogs, so your pets will be an automatic Deal-Breaker. Some nannies will say, "I'm fine with animals, but I don't want to deal with them." Caring for animals—whether it's cats, dogs, hamsters, or turtles—is a completely different job, and many nannies simply don't want to do it. Ultimately, you may either have to pay the nanny a little bit extra to do pet care or make separate arrangements for your animals.

10. Describe a day in the life of your nanny, from the moment she starts in the morning until the end of the day. This is an excellent exercise that will come in very handy when you start conducting your interviews with nanny candidates. You want to talk yourself through the entire day, starting from the time your nanny arrives at work, and write down everything that you normally do and that the nanny will be doing for your child once she starts. To do this, you should think about the main pieces of the *daily* schedule for each child (breakfast at 7:30, school bus at 8:05), and then consider any different *weekly* pieces (karate on Tuesdays, piano on Saturdays). Doing this will give both you and the nanny a really thorough understanding of how your household runs and what you need. For example:

SCHEDULE

- **7 a.m.:** Arrive and say hello to Sophie; she will probably be up and playing
- **7:30 a.m.:** Give her breakfast, usually oatmeal or a bagel and fruit
- **8:00 a.m.:** Do the dishes and tidy up the kitchen while Sophie watches Disney Junior
- **8:15 a.m.:** Help Sophie brush her teeth and get dressed for preschool; she usually chooses her own clothes
- **8:45 a.m.:** Out the door in the stroller to arrive at preschool at 9

If there are any duties you have forgotten, you should go back and add them to the lists you made for questions 2 and 5. When it's time for interviews, you will use what you've come up with to walk your candidates through a typical day and make sure that they understand all the different components of the job. The idea is to give them as much detail as possible and then see how they react.

11. Describe a worst-day scenario in your home. This is the flip side to the day you just described. It's easy for a nanny to be enthusiastic about doing a job where everything always runs like clockwork, but as every parent knows, this almost never happens. This question is designed to help you identify the hardest parts of the job and come up with the real-world, drive-you-crazy, patience-testing scenarios that will challenge your nanny on a daily basis. Once you know what these scenarios are, you can present them to candidates during the interview. How they respond and how they would cope will be very telling. You can also test whether the nanny can handle them during the trials.

To come up with your worst day, simply think about your most trying times as a parent and about the moments in your child's day—such as putting on shoes or brushing teeth—that are likely to set him off and escalate into a full-scale battle. You want to go person by person and hour by hour and list all the things that can go wrong. For example, at breakfast: Two-year-old Tommy throws one of his tantrums because the dog steals a muffin off his plate. Meanwhile, five-year-old Samantha is refusing to get dressed and the kindergarten carpool is coming in ten minutes. The dog throws up everywhere just as the doorbell rings, and Tommy, who is looking for another muffin, tips over a carton of milk.

Doing this exercise also gives you a chance to think *one more time* about the skills you need in a nanny and about what exactly you will be asking her to do. If you have a difficult toddler who throws ten tantrums a day, you don't want to hide this from your candidates. Finding someone who can handle every aspect of your job is critical to making a successful match, and in order to find that person, you need to be frank about the challenges and ask the nanny point-blank, "Can you handle this?" and "How?"

12. Based on all of your previous answers, are there any specific skills that a nanny must have to effectively fulfill her duties and support each child? This is the time to look back over your answers in the Job Duties and Responsibilities section and translate your family's unique needs regarding duties into concrete skills that you can add to your list of job criteria. This list should not include things that any nanny could do, like wash dishes or make beds, but instead focus on the more specific skills that you will have to screen for. Examples would be ability to cook vegetarian (or willingness to learn), ability to organize and manage the children's schedules, ability to read, ability to drive a large SUV and comfortably navigate your neighborhood and surrounding towns, ability to help with second-grade homework, ability to deal with Tommy's tantrums through patience and positive reinforcement.

PART 3: EMOTIONAL JOB DESCRIPTION

Now that you have a clear sense of what your nanny will be doing day to day, it's time to focus on the *personal* qualities you want in a caregiver, and what kind of personality will best suit the different members of your household. This is the time to think about what you and your child need from your nanny, not just in terms of skills and hours, but in an emotional sense: her disposition, her style of care, and how closely she should mirror you as a parent. It's also the time to explore what your "perfect" nanny looks like in terms of her age, appearance, education, and personal history. These are the ad hoc criteria that may or may not have anything to do with how good or capable a nanny actually is, and they may or may not ultimately matter—but they are part of your vision, and your heart is drawn to them just the same.

This part of the FNA is broken down into three sections: Parent Assessment, Child Assessment, and Your Ideal Nanny. Each parent should answer all the questions in section A, and you should answer all the questions in section B separately for each child.

A. Parent Assessment

1. How would you describe your parenting style? This question asks you to think about your own approach to parenting, as well as the tenor and flavor of your household. The three main types of parenting styles are authoritarian, which is extremely rigid; permissive, which is, "We're friends with our children, and don't really have a lot of rules"; and authoritative, which is a balance of both. If you are authoritative, you are casual about some things—for example, what your kids eat or how much TV they watch—but strict about others, such as bedtimes or respect.

Using these three styles as a framework, do your best to articulate your own approach. Do you have a lot of rules or are you more laidback? Do your children have a lot of autonomy or do you like to be involved with everything—from homework to playdates, to what clothes they put on in the morning? Do you feel strongly about discipline, and if so, about which things? Are there certain things you enjoy doing with your children—such as reading or cooking—but others that you prefer to let them do on their own—such as dramatic play or running around outdoors? You want to try to define, as much as you can, how *you* are as a parent so that you can explain it to your candidates.

2. How do you typically interact and communicate with your children? Again, this question is all about articulating your personal style. Are you a very touchy, openly affectionate family with lots of snuggling and hugging every day? Are you very candid when expressing your feelings, whether it's to say, "I love you" or "You are making me very angry"? Do you speak to your children just as you would to a friend or other adult or do you believe in a more formal relationship between parents and children, one based on clear boundaries and respect? The goal is to think about how you typically interact with your children, so that you can describe your communication style to the nanny.

3. Are you looking for someone to replicate your style completely, partner with you fifty–fifty in terms of style, or bring her own style and approach? Now that you've articulated your own style of parenting, it's time to think about what you want from your nanny and how you want *her* to provide care. Many parents end up clashing with their nanny because they don't see eye to eye in terms of how to best care for the child, so now is the time to figure out: Do you want your nanny to be as much like you as possible? Or are you OK with someone who brings a different approach?

Some parents want the nanny to be just like them: If they are huggy and affectionate, they want the nanny to be huggy and affectionate too. If they like to be goofy and joke around with their kids, they want a nanny who brings that same playfulness and sense of humor. But there are also a lot of parents who want a nanny to provide some balance and come to the table with her own philosophy and ideas. Some parents want a nanny with a totally different style— for example, they might be very relaxed with their kids, but want a nanny who will be more organized and strict. One mom would always tell me, "I loved how my last nanny would just look at my boys and they would immediately hop to." She liked that the nanny was stronger and firmer than she was, because she felt it was better for two rowdy preschoolers.

This series of questions asks you to think about the ideal balance of "yours" and "hers" when it comes to childcare and to identify any specific ways in which you would like the nanny to mirror your approach. If you want someone to replicate you 100 percent, you will need to pinpoint exactly what it is that you want her to replicate, whether it's your calm demeanor, your views on sleep training, or your preference for educational activities in daily play. If you're hoping to learn from your nanny and are looking for more of a fifty–fifty partnership, you will need to spell out the ways in which you want her to be like you, along with the areas where she can do things her way and take the lead. Even if you want your nanny to do things completely differently, you will still need to articulate what type of style and approach you want so that you can assess for it during interviews and trials.

Once you've answered these questions, you should have a very good idea of the exact balance that you're looking for, and therefore be able to be extremely clear with candidates during interviews. For example, you might say, "We're always open to hearing about new ways or better ways of doing things, but the one thing we are strict about is keeping the kids on a schedule, and we need mealtimes, naptimes, and bedtimes to remain the same."

4. Are there any specific positions on childrearing that you would like your nanny to have or not have? This is where you want to think specifically about the positions you hold on childrearing—breast vs. bottle, Ferber method vs. crying it out, schedule vs. feeding on demand, time-outs vs. positive reinforcement—because there will inevitably be nannies who are supportive of your choices, and nannies who are not. You don't want her administering "tough love" to your toddler, or battling with your twelve-year-old daughter over how she dresses if that isn't your approach, so you want to identify your specific views early on so that you can explain them to the nanny and make sure she is on board. This will also help prevent any misunderstandings during trials. I had one client who was furious after a trial because the nanny had let the baby cry for ten minutes. But when I spoke to the nanny, she said, "I just came from a family who believed in hardcore sleep training, and they would have fired me if I'd gone in to get the child after less than ten minutes." Nannies will often automatically do whatever they did for their last employer, so you don't want to rule out someone who may be perfectly willing to do things your way, if you just take the time to explain what you want.

5. Have you ever employed a childcare provider before? This question asks you to reflect on any past experiences you've had with other caregivers—whether it was a nanny, an au pair, a baby nurse, or even a babysitter—and to identify the things that worked well and did *not* work well in each scenario. You might say, "I liked that she was totally honest, I liked the way we communicated, and I liked that she put the baby on a schedule. But I didn't like that she talked on the phone all the time, and I didn't like that she was almost never available to stay late." The question gives you another opportunity to translate your past experiences into a very clear list of likes and dislikes, and get clear about what you want from your next nanny.

6. Are there any practices or behaviors that are Deal-Breakers for you? This question is designed to help you pinpoint the practices and behaviors that are unacceptable in your house and about which you intend to draw a hard line. Essentially, they are your biggest, most important rules. Everyone's Deal-Breakers are different; I have had mothers who were so focused on punctuality that they canceled a trial when the candidate was two minutes late, and other mothers who didn't mind if the nanny was late as long as she did the job well. Other issues like cell phone use, watching TV when your children are around, snacks, exercise, and bringing their own kids to the job matter a lot to some families but not to others. Of course the big ones are yelling at a child, ignoring a child, lying, stealing, cursing, and any form of physical or verbal abuse. Whatever you feel strongly about, your nanny needs to know just *how* strongly you feel up front, and you need to present these issues to her in the interview as definite Deal-Breakers—no excuses.

7. Do you mind if your nanny has young children of her own? A nanny's own children and family life may or may not affect her ability to do your job. It is most often a problem if the nanny has very young children, because she will likely have less flexibility in her schedule in terms of staying late or working weekends, and she may require more sick or personal days. If you are someone who needs maximum flexibility because you work irregular hours or your children have chaotic schedules, you will need to address this during the interview. If the nanny has other family to watch her children or has made some other arrangement, overtime and weekend hours may not be a problem. If she has older children, it may actually be a plus because she will have been through all of the developmental stages as a mother.

8. Based on your answers to questions 1–7, list the personal qualities and characteristics that you are most looking for in a nanny. Now that you've completed your Parent Assessment, you should review your answers and try to translate them into a list of the *personal* qualities you most want in a nanny. What are your conclusions in terms of style of caregiving, personality, values, positions on childrearing, and personal background? Once you have your list, you will have defined the most important pieces of *your* ideal, emotional match.

B. Child Assessment

9. What are your child's current developmental needs? Now that you've identified your own emotional needs, it's time to think about those of your child. Your child is the most important person in your world, so you want to take the time to really assess what he requires from a nanny or other caregiver at this particular point in his life. If your child is older, he may come to this process with his own ready-made set of likes and dislikes. But in addition to thinking about what he wants, it's important to think about what he needs from a purely developmental perspective—that is, what type of interaction and stimulation will best foster his optimum social, emotional, and cognitive growth.

The science of early childhood development tells us that all children pass through the same stages as they grow: infancy, early childhood (also known as the toddler years), preschool, school age, and adolescence. It also tells us that the type of care they receive at each stage determines whether they will grow up to be happy, well-adjusted adults. The chart below is based on the work of psychologist Erik Erikson and is designed to help you know exactly what your child needs from his caregivers at every age, whether the caregiver is a parent, a nanny, or another type of childcare professional. You should use it to determine your child's most fundamental needs at this time as well as to help you evaluate potential nannies.

DEVELOPMENTAL STAGE: Infancy (Birth to 18 Months)

THIS STAGE IS ABOUT...

Trust vs. Mistrust
Children master this stage by developing trust in their caregiver and the world. Trust is gained by receiving constant, reliable physical care and emotional affection.

GOLD STANDARD CAREGIVER REQUIREMENTS
Your child needs extremely positive, attentive caregivers who hold, soothe, rock, talk, and sing. The caregiver's face should be warm,

happy, adoring, and expressive. When walking begins, the caregiver must possess great energy and enthusiasm for this new mobility.

OUTCOME OF A POOR CAREGIVER

If a caregiver is slow to respond when your child cries or to attend to his needs (like changing diapers), or has a bland, detached demeanor, your child will feel unsafe and mistrustful of the world. That inability to feel safe will affect his ability to learn and grow.

DEVELOPMENTAL STAGE: Early Childhood (2–3 Years)

THIS STAGE IS ABOUT . . .

Autonomy vs. Shame and Doubt
At this stage, children are learning to develop a sense of independence and personal control over their physical skills (such as walking or toilet training). Success and positive reinforcement lead to autonomy; failure results in feelings of shame and doubt.

GOLD STANDARD CAREGIVER REQUIREMENTS

Caregivers at this stage need to have extreme positive energy, mobility, and patience. They must be able to provide physical stimulation through games and play, educational stimulation through reading and talking, and physical safety by being quick on their feet. Toddlers require a caregiver who is fit and healthy, always five steps ahead, and who can anticipate their movements so they don't get hurt. Caregivers also need to be able to set limits calmly, while still supporting the "I can do it myself" attitude.

OUTCOME OF A POOR CAREGIVER

If a caregiver is lazy, tired, or gets annoyed or angry when the child tries to be autonomous (such as running in the park, making a mess, or exploring with hands and mouth), the child will learn, "If I try new things, I upset people." If a caregiver prevents exploration by strapping him in a stroller or confining him in a playpen, his development will be physically and emotionally stunted.

DEVELOPMENTAL STAGE: Preschool (3–5 Years)

THIS STAGE IS ABOUT...

Initiative vs. Guilt

Children need to begin asserting power and control over their environment. Success at this stage leads to a sense of purpose. Children who try to exert too much power experience disapproval, which results in a sense of guilt.

GOLD STANDARD CAREGIVER REQUIREMENTS

As with early childhood, caregivers must be able to teach while preventing physical and educational boredom. They must be able to create and execute fun activities such as doing crafts, reading books, baking, or playing sports games. Teaching emotional skills such as kindness, compassion, and care for others, as well as manners and respect, is crucial at this stage.

OUTCOME OF A POOR CAREGIVER

Caregivers need to praise and reinforce the child's initiative in wanting to do or create something, but this requires time, care, patience, and guidance from the adult to see it through. If a caregiver is lazy or rigid and doesn't want to try something different, do the art project, or play the game, the child will feel guilty for trying to assert control, and will ultimately stop asking and thinking of new things to do.

DEVELOPMENTAL STAGE: School Age (6–11 Years)

THIS STAGE IS ABOUT...

Industry vs. Inferiority

At this stage, children need to cope with new social and academic demands. Success leads to a sense of confidence, while failure results in feelings of inferiority.

GOLD STANDARD CAREGIVER REQUIREMENTS

Entering school is the major adjustment at this stage, and children will need help with homework, guidance on social situations, and help learning how to think positively. Unless there is a parent at home, or at home part-time, a nanny must be able to handle these issues—from academic challenges to fights with friends.

OUTCOME OF A POOR CAREGIVER

Your child will struggle if there is no one supporting him at home or no one noticing a problem at school. If the caregiver is tired and doesn't want to be bothered or won't allow time to talk and engage with your child about the science experiment or watch the new gymnastics routine, your child will lose confidence. Having no one to support and foster his industry leads him to feel inferior.

DEVELOPMENTAL STAGE: Adolescence (12–18 Years)

THIS STAGE IS ABOUT . . .

Identity vs. Role Confusion

Teens need to develop a sense of self and personal identity. Success leads to an ability to stay true to yourself, while failure leads to role confusion and a weak sense of self.

GOLD STANDARD CAREGIVER REQUIREMENTS

The caregiver needs to be understanding, loving, stable, and warm so that a teen can seek support after a tough day at school. They also need to have the strength to stand up to a teen about household rules such as drinking, drugs, and curfews when the parents are not there. Compassion and social guidance are key.

OUTCOME OF A POOR CAREGIVER

Tweens and teens will spiral out of control if problems at school are coupled with poor caregiving at home. If a caregiver is too busy or distracted to offer support or unable to provide emotional care such

as reinforcing values and positive messages about self-worth, the
teen will feel as lost at home as he does at school.

10. Describe the caregiver personality best suited to your child. Using the chart above along with your own knowledge of your child, try
to articulate the style of caregiver best suited to support your child's
developmental and emotional needs. If your child is shy and sensitive,
she might do well with someone who is very gentle and loving—or
you might feel that she needs someone with a more extroverted nature
who can try to coax your child out of her shell. If your child is very
active and adventurous, you will likely need someone who can match
her energy and is willing to try new things. If you have a difficult
child who is prone to throwing tantrums to assert her independence,
you will need a nanny who is very strong and patient and knows how
to set firm limits. The key is to consider not only what your child
would want but what type of nanny will best help your child to grow
and thrive.

**11. If your child is older, how does he or she feel about having a new
nanny?** The idea here is to think about the ways in which your child's
feelings about having a new caregiver might affect or impede the
process. For example, if you have a child who hates to be around new
people, and you know she is going to give any nanny a hard time, you
need to acknowledge that this is something that is going to make trials, as well as the first few weeks on the job, challenging. Or if your
tween is still heartbroken over the loss of her last nanny, you know
that is she is likely to be distrustful of anybody new. Recognizing
these issues now will enable you to explain them to your candidates
up front and find out exactly how they would cope with or handle
your child's emotions. It also prepares the nanny for whatever she
may encounter on the job or during the trial, so that together you can
devise a strategy for making the situation work.

C. Your Ideal Nanny

12. What does the ideal candidate look like for your family? This question helps you sum up your Emotional Job Description by asking you to create a profile of your ideal nanny based on the preferences you identified in questions 1–11. Your answers should focus on the nanny's personality, style of caregiving, and personal background rather than on specific professional skills. The profile also asks you to consider additional characteristics that parents often feel strongly about, such as age, personal appearance, and religion, and how they may or may not matter to your search. You should go through each of the suggested topics on the FNA form and write down what you think you want, and why. Again, there are no wrong answers here— the purpose of the exercise is to come up with an honest picture of the nanny you feel would be your ideal emotional match.

Age. I always tell my clients that age as a number often has very little significance when it comes to nannies. Instead, what you should assess for, depending on the needs of your child, is energy, physicality, and an ability to meet his developmental needs. Young children, especially toddlers and high-energy preschoolers, need someone active who can keep up with them all day long. But while it might make sense to try to hire someone younger, age alone does not guarantee that a nanny will be willing to creatively and actively engage your child. You can have a twenty-five-year-old nanny who is inactive and checked out, while my own nanny, Maria, is in her sixties and has three times the energy that I do. Similarly, age alone is not a predictor of experience: A nanny may be in her fifties and have been a nanny for thirty years, but that doesn't mean that she is a terrific nanny or that she will be a better fit for your family than someone newer to the profession. If age is something you think you feel strongly about, remember to keep an open mind and focus on qualities rather than the number.

Experience. The most important experience that any nanny can have is the kind that relates directly to your nanny position—for example, if you have twins and she's worked with twins before, or if you are both full-time working parents and she is used to that. The kind of experience that doesn't matter—but that many parents end up focusing on—is how long she has been a professional nanny (if she's only a mediocre nanny, twenty years of experience doesn't matter) and whether or not the nanny has worked for some well-known family (plenty of well-known, wealthy families hire lousy nannies, trust me). As you think about this question, make sure that you are prioritizing the *right* kinds of experience, and do your best to pinpoint exactly what kind will enable a nanny to be successful at *your* job. And remember that you can't look at someone's résumé alone—you have to see her in action during a trial.

Education. Some parents make a big deal about education, but in my opinion, how much it matters really depends on your situation. There are many wonderful nannies who have never been to college or may have never even finished high school, but they are still loving, attentive caregivers who excel at playing and engaging with children and at teaching them basic things like manners and ABCs. Especially with babies and very young children, my feeling is that formal education doesn't matter nearly as much as the quality of the emotional nurturing and physical care.

That said, in some cases, a certain level of education may be necessary to meet your child's developmental needs. If your children are older and need a parental unit nanny who can help them out with more advanced homework and school projects when the parents are not there, or you have a highly intelligent, precocious young child who requires a lot of learning-based stimulation to keep him entertained, then educational background may be a factor in who you hire. But it should never be the most important factor, because if the love and emotional connection between a nanny and child are not there, your child may be learning, but he won't be getting what he needs.

Cultural Background. Many parents come to the table with a host of preconceived notions—good and bad—about nannies from different cultures and the type of care they will provide. For every parent I have who is afraid to hire nannies from a certain culture, I have another parent who is obsessed with a particular ethnic background and thinks that Tibetan nannies—or British nannies or Jamaican nannies—are the only acceptable choice. In the nanny world, cultural stereotypes abound. While people from certain cultures do tend to possess certain cultural traits, my advice for parents has always been: When it comes to generalizations, don't believe the bad ones and don't buy into the promise of the good ones—it's all about the individual. Unless you have a very specific, legitimate reason for avoiding or wanting a nanny from a particular culture, I advise you to keep an open mind, evaluate each candidate individually, and cast as wide a net as possible.

Language Skills. We've already talked about foreign language skills, but how much should you care about English competency? In my experience, some parents go way overboard on this, and others don't prioritize it enough. Many nannies don't speak perfect, fluent English, but no matter what people may tell you, a nanny's imperfect grammar is *not* going to affect your child. If that were the case, we would have millions of kids walking around all over the country with foreign accents different from their parents'.

There are, however, several areas where you do need to think about and screen for language competency. The first one is reading: Can the nanny read a book? It doesn't have to be Proust or Dostoyevsky, but children love to read, and reading builds both language and cognitive skills, so you will need to make sure that your nanny can at least read board books and picture books during your child's formative years. The second is the ability to handle medications and communicate in an emergency, because if you have a parental unit nanny, these duties are going to be required. The third is the ability to help with homework if that is something you want your nanny to do. If a nanny can't do homework, you can always hire a tutor or do it yourself when you get home.

Far more worrisome than a nanny who speaks with an accent is having a nanny who doesn't speak *enough*. A child isn't going to learn words if the nanny isn't speaking words *to* him, and this can cause a language delay. So when it comes to the nanny's language skills, don't worry about perfect English; the most important thing is to have a nanny who talks readily and profusely and engages your child in conversation.

Personality. Based on your answers to questions 1–11, describe your ideal nanny personality. Keep in mind that if different members of your household have different preferences, the person who will be interacting with the nanny the most—whether that's you or your child—should take priority. If the father wants someone who is going to be very quiet and unobtrusive, but he's at the office all week long, his wishes shouldn't rule the day. However, if he's working from home, and he's going to be managing the nanny most of the time in terms of directing, communicating, and paying her every week, then his wishes do need to carry weight. Similarly, if both parents are gone all day, the most important thing is finding a nanny who will be an ideal personality match for your child. If your child loves the nanny, and she loves him and meets all of his developmental needs, you don't need to have a deep connection with her but simply a pleasant, professional working relationship.

Communication Style. To answer this question, think about times in your personal and professional life when you've communicated with different parties and what type of communication works best for you. Some people just want to be the employer and to give the nanny directions and have things get done, but some people want more of a collaboration, where you speak as equals, give each other feedback, and discuss how to handle certain situations with your child. You also need to think about how *much* communication you want to have: Do you want text message updates and pictures throughout the day? Or are you too busy at work to deal with that, so an end-of-day or even once-a-week recap is fine with you? There are moms who say, "I want the nanny to ask me before she does anything," and there are moms who say, "I just can't handle a million questions; I really need someone who can first try to figure it out, and then come to me if she still needs help." The key is to first think about how *you* want to communicate, and then articulate the style of communication that you need from your nanny.

Appearance. Some parents care a lot about a nanny's personal appearance because they feel that their nanny is a role model for their children. They tell me, "If she doesn't have a neat appearance, I don't want to hire her." But nannies are not going to work at a fancy office. They're rolling around on the floor, making art projects, playing in the sandbox, getting spilled on, and sometimes doing chores and housework. Many nannies choose to dress purely for comfort, and that's OK. My feeling is that unless your children are older, you don't want to hire someone who's so put together that she's not willing to play trucks in the dirt because she might get mud on her outfit. You want your nanny to be comfortable and able to do her job without distraction. That said, if you have strong feelings about personal appearance—for example, you don't want tattoos and piercings—you have a right to screen for whatever you want. But if it is casualness or frumpiness you're worried about, think about what the job requires and worry about something else.

Religion. Religion can be a sensitive subject for many people, but it's one that bears thinking about when it comes to nannies. If your nanny is very religious or makes religious references or talks about Bible stories with your children, is that something that is going to bother you? This is one issue that almost never comes up in a traditional nanny search but can present big problems if it doesn't get addressed. If you feel strongly that your child only have a certain type of religious influence, you should ask a nanny about her beliefs during the interview and make your wishes known: "We respect all religious viewpoints, but we really want our beliefs to be respected in our home." Or "We are responsible for our child's spiritual upbringing, and we would prefer that you not discuss religion with our children at all."

13. What are the best aspects of the position and working for your family? Any nanny that you talk to is going to want to know the answer to this question, so take some time now to think about the position and the advantages of working for you. Some examples are good pay, good hours, a relaxed atmosphere, convenient to public transportation, you're looking to partner with the nanny, you are extremely supportive and respectful employers, your children are friendly and easy to work with, and you really value kindness as a family.

14. What do you think will be the most difficult aspects of the position and working for your family? This question can be hard for people to answer, but it's important to be aware of the challenges of the position so that you can be frank with your candidates and find someone who is up to the task. Some things you might want to mention are long hours, the number of children, the amount of duties for the job, a more strict or rigid household with a lot of rules, or pay below the competitive rate. You need to know what the disadvantages are so that you can counter with the advantages: "We know that our salary is below the competitive rate, but this is all we can afford, and we are an extremely loving and supportive family; we treat our nanny as one of us."

15. What may be difficult for a new nanny coming into your home, and what skills might help the nanny with this transition? This question helps you connect a nanny's personality traits to the most challenging aspects of your job. If you know that your toddler is going to be a handful or your teenager is initially going to be mistrustful and obnoxious, you know that you will need someone with a thick skin. Or if you live in a very big house and you know it's going to be exhausting running up and down three flights of stairs and corralling three kids and getting them into the car and where they need to be, you know that someone who is not active and tires easily is going to have trouble adapting. Or if your daughter is very sensitive and cries at the littlest thing, a nanny may need to be extremely gentle and have a good deal of patience to manage her. This is an opportunity to think specifically about the skills that will help a nanny counteract the hard parts of the job.

PART 4: SUMMING UP

Now it's time to review and compile all of your findings and answers into three important lists that you will use as you go forward in the process: the Musts, Pluses, and Deal-Breakers for your job.

1. Based on all of the information you've gathered from the previous questions, list the Must Haves for the position. Starting with the Physical Job Description section, read through your answers and pick out your Musts—that is, the job parameters (like hours, days, and travel), skills, personality traits, and personal characteristics that you absolutely can't live without. Try to be as reasonable about your Musts as you can and list only the ones that are not negotiable, no matter what. Having too many Musts can narrow your pool and curtail your search. I recommend dividing your list into physical Musts (from the first two parts of the FNA) and emotional Musts (from the third part).

> *Examples:* physical Musts: Monday to Friday, 7 a.m. to 6 p.m., drives; emotional Musts: has worked with a stay-at-home mom, experience with toddlers.

2. Now list the Pluses—skills and abilities that would be nice to have, but are not essential. Anything else that you really want goes on this list: French speaking, vegetarian, artistic, college educated, experience with tweens . . . whatever you want.

> *Examples:* cooks, speaks Spanish, can swim.

3. And finally, list your Deal-Breakers. This is your unique list of rules that are nonnegotiable. You will use this list throughout the search process, particularly when you check references and do interviews.

> *Examples:* no cell phone, no being late.

Congratulations—you finished! You put in the time, you did the work, and now you have a clear vision of what your own Gold Standard nanny looks like. You also have three handy checklists to help you advertise, explain your position, and screen potential candidates. You're one step closer to finding your perfect nanny, so let's move on to talk about how to find and make contact with potential candidates in the next stage of the hiring process: Basic Screening.

CHAPTER 4

———

Basic Screening

Finding Candidates
Who Meet Your Needs

Now that you've completed your Family Needs Assessment and identified the Musts and Pluses for your nanny position, it's time to make contact with potential candidates. This stage of my Gold Standard hiring process involves finding nannies and putting them through what I call Basic Screening. Basic Screening is a quick way to assess whether a candidate meets your needs and flesh out her background information a bit more so that you can decide if she is a truly viable prospect. The idea is to weed out unqualified candidates right away so that you don't waste time checking references or meeting with someone who can't actually work the hours you need, or who doesn't match the other basic criteria for your job.

Finding Candidates

The Gold Standard strategy for finding great candidates boils down to two simple rules: First, never use only one source, and second, make contact with as many nannies as possible. You want to cast a wide net because even if you start with a list of twenty potential candidates, as soon as you start your Basic Screening and Reference Checks, that list of twenty will quickly whittle down to fifteen, then ten, and by the time you get to interviews you may have only five applicants who match your list of Musts and Pluses. Fortunately, there are many different resources for finding candidates, including agencies, websites, message boards, word of mouth, and targeted advertising based on your family's FNA. Let's take a closer look at each of these channels, and at how to best take advantage of what they offer.

NANNY AGENCIES

Working with a nanny agency can be a good way to gain immediate access to a large pool of candidates, provided that you don't mind the cost. A nanny agency will typically charge an intake/registration fee of several hundred dollars, and then, if you hire one of their nannies, 12 to 20 percent of the nanny's annual salary. The pluses to working with an agency are that you'll have someone to assist you and a ready supply of different candidates—if you don't like the first five nannies they send you, they can send you five more the very next day. The downside is that, in my experience, agencies often overpromise and underdeliver. Even if they tell you that a candidate has been background checked, these checks can be extremely unreliable, and there is often very little thought put into matching a nanny with a family.

Most important, the fee—even at the toniest agencies—*does not* guarantee quality. Remember, the nanny world is the Wild West, and agencies aren't regulated any more than the nannies are. Smaller local agencies in particular have a propensity for shady activity, and I have encountered several such agencies in my career that provided nannies with forged documents and fake driver's licenses. So you need to keep in mind that just because a nanny comes to you through an agency, it does *not* mean that she is guaranteed to be legal, more competent, more qualified, or of sounder mind than a nanny you would find elsewhere. You should still put the candidates through all the steps of the Gold Standard hiring process (call the references, do in-home trials) to make sure that you are getting what you pay for. My steps and techniques combined with an agency's database and services can be a very effective combination.

PAID ONLINE DATABASES

The term *online database* refers to subscription websites like Care .com, Sittercity.com, UrbanSitter.com, eNannySource.com, and many others. Like agencies, these websites give you immediate access to a sizable pool of candidates—but unlike agencies, they don't charge a hefty placement fee. Instead, for a much smaller fee, you can post an ad for your job and search for local caregivers using a number of filters such as language, hourly rate, and experience. It's important to know that while many of these websites will say that a candidate has been background checked or offer background checks for an additional fee, there are many different levels of background checks, and many will not be thorough enough to catch a crime committed by a nanny at a previous address, in another state, or under a former name. You should be prepared to run your own background checks on anyone you want to hire from one of these websites (more about how to do this on page 145).

PAID ADVERTISING IN LOCAL NEWSPAPERS

Ethnic newspapers in particular can be a great way to target a particular group of nannies, such as Spanish-speaking nannies or Russian nannies, depending on what you're looking for. You can also try placing ads in smaller publications, such as college newspapers, town or neighborhood circulars, or church bulletins.

FREE POSTING BOARDS AND WEBSITES

You can post an ad for your job for free and browse potential candidates on websites like Craigslist.com, Backpage.com, and Mommy bites.com as well as community message boards, local online mommy groups, and forums for working mothers. In general, the postings from nannies on these sites will be shorter, less polished, and less detailed than the ones on paid sites like Care.com, but this does not automatically mean that the nanny who posts on Craigslist is less

---

HOW TO CREATE AN AD FOR YOUR POSITION

One very effective way to source potential candidates is to create a highly specific ad for your job that invites qualified nannies to come to you. Rather than scrolling through hundreds of listings and trying to guess which nannies will be a fit for your job, an ad allows you to define your criteria up front so that you will automatically narrow down the number of responses and attract a self-selected pool of interested people.

The Gold Standard strategy for writing an ad is to be *as specific as possible*. Using the information gleaned from your FNA, you should include all of your Musts and Pluses and describe what's good or advantageous about working for your family. Don't worry about the number of words in the ad because the time you save in the long run by being detailed now will be worth it. *Do not* specify salary or specific rates, as they should be discussed later; however, if you can pay at or above the competitive rate, or offer good benefits like health insurance, it is worth mentioning in the ad, especially if the job is challenging with many children or long hours. It is also a good idea to state "Background check required." I recommend setting up a new email account to use in your posting so that your regular email isn't flooded with responses.

Sample Ad

> Terrific family in South City, NY, looking for full-time, live-in nanny to take care of two children (3 months and 2 years old). Hours are Monday–Friday from 7:00 a.m. to 7:00 p.m. with flexibility to stay late one night a week. Must have at least one year of full-time experience as a live-in nanny, heavy infant experience, a valid driver's license, and two references from past nanny jobs that we can speak to. Must have legal working papers and be able to travel internationally for four weeks a year with the family. Must read, write, and speak English fluently; French speaking a plus, but not a must. College degree a plus, but not a must. Duties will include light housekeeping and cooking for children. Must be affectionate, fun loving, and enjoy being outdoors. Private bedroom with bath, excellent salary, and happy, energetic kids! Respond only if you meet *all* of the requirements to mom@southcityny.com. Background check required.

qualified or wonderful than the one who posts on Sittercity—it may simply mean that, like many nannies, English is not her first language and she is not comfortable with computers. When using these sites, you need to be able to look past the typos and occasional spelling errors and try to get a sense of what the person has to offer. Parents will also use these sites to post ads for their former nannies to try to help them find a new job. It goes without saying that a parent-placed ad is a big plus for any candidate because it means she already has a willing reference.

FREE POSTING AT PUBLIC LOCATIONS

You can post a written ad for your nanny job anywhere that it might be seen by potential nannies, including college career centers, child development centers, nursing schools, libraries, churches and synagogues, kids' gyms, popular indoor play spaces, and preschools.

FREE REFERRALS THROUGH
FRIENDS AND NEIGHBORS

One of the best ways to find candidates is by networking with friends and friends of friends who have nannies because any nanny you find through these channels will likely come with a personal recommendation as well as some context about her previous employer. You should ask all the parents you know to put the word out and talk to your colleagues, neighbors, doorman, pediatrician, and any other nannies you know to see if they have a recommendation.

Screening Your Candidates

Once you begin receiving responses to your ad and finding postings by nannies that you are interested in, it's time to begin the screening process. Your starting point for Basic Screening will be different with each candidate, depending on how you found them. If they came to you through an agency, or you spotted their profile on Care.com, you may already have a fairly detailed work history and résumé. But if they were referred to you through a friend or simply responded to your ad, you are going to need to ask for details about their background and experience to get a sense of who they are and what they bring to the table. The idea is to come away from Basic Screening with not only a clear sense of whether a nanny meets your specific needs but a complete overview of her professional experience along with employer names and contact information, so that you can immediately move on to the next step: Reference Checks.

Basic Screening should be done over the phone so that you can get a sense of the nanny's language skills. There are, unfortunately, nannies who will have their husbands or children respond to ads and emails for them, and who, when you finally meet them in person, have very poor English skills. With an executor nanny, this may not matter, but if strong language skills are a Must for your job, and the nanny is going to be left alone with your children, it's best to do the screen over the phone so that you can assess the nanny's ability to communicate as soon as possible.

SCREENING CHEAT SHEET: CREATING A BASIC SCREENING WORKSHEET

Before you begin reaching out to candidates, I recommend creating your own Basic Screening Worksheet that you can use to guide your conversation with each candidate and keep track of how she responds. The first two sections of the worksheet should be your lists of Musts and Pluses from your FNA so that you can easily run through them with the nanny and check off the ones she meets. The third section should be a space where you can compile information about her previous employers and make notes about the details of her past jobs, including the contact information for her references. The last section should be the nanny's desired salary: When you press her to reveal her number, what does she say? When you finish, you should have a completed worksheet for each candidate that contains all of her essential information and allows you to compare and evaluate the different candidates side by side.

SCREENING STEP 1: CONFIRM
THE MUSTS OF YOUR JOB

The first and most important step in Basic Screening is to confirm the Musts for your nanny position. When you get the candidate on the phone, review your lists of Musts from your FNA and make sure that she meets all of your basic requirements. This is also the time to explain some of the basic details of the position, including duties and number of children. This way, you give the nanny a clear picture of what the job entails and confirm that she is still interested in moving forward. Remember that nannies are interviewing you as much as you are interviewing them, so you want to be pleasant and friendly throughout the conversation. Don't be afraid to ask for further clarification if the nanny says something that you don't understand or to politely cut the call short if it becomes clear that she doesn't match the key criteria for the job.

SCREENING STEP 2: ASSESS FOR ANY ADDITIONAL
PLUSES

If a nanny confirms that she meets all of your Musts, you can then move on to see whether she also meets any of your Pluses. While Pluses may not be necessary to do the job, assessing for them now will help you to rank the candidates who make it through Basic Screening and decide who to prioritize going forward.

SCREENING STEP 3: CREATE A NANNY TIMELINE

Once you've confirmed that the candidate meets your essential job criteria, it's time to ask for more information about her professional experience. You can start by asking, "Can you walk me through your

work history? Tell me about each of the families you've worked for."
As you listen to her response, you want to be on the lookout for any
gaps in her résumé that she can't explain, or long periods of time
between jobs. A good timeline would be this: "I came to America in
2003 and worked for the Smiths for six years. They had two children,
a boy and a girl, and I cared for them from the time they were born
until they were both in school and didn't need a nanny anymore.
Then I worked for the Greens for four years, they had a little girl who
I cared for from the time she was one, and I left that position because
the father got a different job and they had to move." A more suspect
timeline is this: "I came to America in 2003 and worked for the
Smiths for a year and a half, then I went to work in a bank but I didn't
like it, so I went to work for the Greens, but I didn't like working for
them, the kids were crazy, so I went to work for the Millers." If someone has bounced around a lot or alternated nanny positions with
other jobs, you will need to do some digging with both the nanny and
her references to figure out the real story.

Good nannies should have nothing to hide, so they shouldn't
have any problem answering questions about the kind of work they
did for each family, where they got the "toddler experience" listed in
their profile, or what they were doing between nanny jobs. If you
sense any sort of defensiveness or impatience with your questions,
consider it a red flag.

SCREENING STEP 4: ESTABLISH
THE NANNY'S REQUIRED SALARY

Now that you have reviewed your Musts and gotten an overview of
the nanny's professional history, it's time to raise the issue of salary.
The Gold Standard strategy for discussing money with your candidates is simple: *Don't reveal exactly what you are willing to pay until*

you are ready to make an offer. This is because what you ultimately decide to offer will depend somewhat on the nanny you want to hire. You may start out thinking that you want to pay $600, but then find someone so amazing that you are willing to stretch to your limit of $800. Your chosen nanny may have additional skills that command more money or she may be open to working for a lower rate because she lives nearby and doesn't have to commute. You don't want to be locked into a number—high or low—until you've determined what any given nanny is worth to your family by meeting with her, trialing her, and assessing what she brings to the table. That said, you also don't want to waste your time on someone who is totally beyond your price range (for tips on figuring out your ideal salary, see page 56). The key is to raise the issue of salary during Basic Screening but to do so in a way that forces the nanny to reveal *her* magic number, without revealing yours. Here's how it works:

• **Ask the nanny, "Can you tell me, knowing our job parameters, what is the minimum weekly salary that you would need to do this job?"** This way, you put the nanny on the spot and force her to say a number. For example, she may say, "I've been a nanny for ten years, and to do that job, I'd need seven hundred fifty." If $750 falls within your salary range, then you know that you have a viable candidate and you can move her forward in the process.

If $750 is more than you can afford, you can say, "I'm sorry, but $750 is nowhere near what we can do" or "That's much higher than we were thinking," and see if the nanny budges. If she was bluffing or really needs the job she may say, "OK, I can wiggle a little bit, let's keep meeting." If you really like the candidate—she seems to have everything you want—you can also say, "That's higher than we were thinking, but we might be able to get closer to that number. Knowing that, would you be willing to go through the process and test our family out?" And then you can decide, based on her references, interview, and trials, whether this particular nanny is worth the stretch. A lot of nannies know that you can't put a price on a good family, so they may come down a bit if they get a good feeling about you during a trial. But if $750 is a hard-line number and there's no way that you can meet it, it's best to find out as soon as possible and move on.

If the nanny refuses to give you a number, and instead turns it around and asks, "What are you looking to pay?" You should answer, "We don't really know what we're paying yet. We're going to figure it out as we go through the process, and we're going to base it on experience and education and what a nanny brings to our family in terms of skills. So I'd like to hear what you think you'd need to do the job. This isn't something we're going to hold you to; we just need to know if we're in the right ballpark."

There are a lot of nannies who won't give you an exact number but will say that they are "willing to be flexible"—and that's a good thing! You can move forward with the nanny knowing that you have someone who, if she likes the job and your family, is open to finding common ground. When you get to the interview, you can try to tease out that number again by using the same strategy.

• **If the nanny tries to talk about an hourly wage, gently steer her back to weekly.** There are some nannies who will gloss over your request for a weekly rate and instead quote you an hourly one. "For that job, I would need sixteen dollars an hour." If that happens, you just explain, "We're not going to be doing hourly; we're really looking at the week—and it's for both of our benefits. Because if we have fewer hours one week, you won't be getting what you need, and we've been told that *it's much more fair to the nanny* to pay a weekly wage because you should know that you are guaranteed a certain amount in salary each week. Otherwise you may tally one number of hours and I may tally another, and this way, you know that you will be paid the same rate no matter what." You also want to make it clear that the weekly rate will apply to the basic parameters you've set—a certain set of hours on certain days—and that for anything beyond that, the nanny will be paid overtime.

The majority of nannies will agree to this, because they will recognize that an hourly wage can be unstable. If the nanny says no, or tries to tell you, "Oh no, we nannies always do it by the hour," know that it isn't true, and simply say, "Well, I'm afraid we can't do it then," and let her go. Unless you're OK with paying more and don't mind the responsibility of tracking hours, you will do better with someone who respects your wishes and is willing to accept what you have to offer.

• **Ask her what she made at her last few jobs.** References are a great way to find out the truth about what a nanny is used to making, so you should plan to confirm whatever rate a nanny quotes you with her previous employer during your reference checks. You should ask, "Would you mind telling me what you made when you started with these families, and what you were being paid when you left?" Once you know what the nanny made at her last job, you can use those numbers as a benchmark for what you can expect to pay. Some nannies will be OK with going back to their former starting salary, even if they did a great job and were raised to a higher rate, and some nannies will feel that whatever they made at the end of the last job is where they should start and won't accept less than that number. Either way, you now have a sense of her range, which will be helpful when it's time to negotiate.

SCREENING STEP 5: OBTAIN HER LIST OF REFERENCES

At the end of the call, it's time to say, "I'd like to call your references before we meet for an interview. Can you please provide me with the contact information for these families?" A nanny may not have the contact information for every set of parents at her fingertips, and that's OK, as long as she is willing to track it down and get back to you as soon as possible. For any candidate to move on to the next round, you need to have at least one checkable reference and preferably more. If she has four previous jobs but provides you with a phone number and email for only one family, she needs to be able to explain why.

Assessing What You've Learned

Once you have completed your initial screening, it's time to review all the information and decide whether you want to move forward with the candidate. Here are some questions to consider:

- Does she fulfill all your Musts and meet your general expectations?
- Did you feel good about your brief interaction with her? Was she pleasant and willing to answer your questions?
- Is the information that she gave you over the phone consistent with what is on her résumé or in her online profile?
- Does her work history show that she has a good track record of staying with families and that childcare is her profession of choice?
- Has she provided you with checkable references?

Keep in mind as you assess your candidates that Basic Screening is *not* a good indicator of a nanny's personality. Most nannies, especially those who speak English as a second language, are not going to be incredibly dynamic and personable over the phone. They're often nervous, and they may say almost nothing aside from answering your questions. The nanny should seem pleasant and polite and be able to communicate clearly, but don't worry if she doesn't wow you during this first call. Instead, check with her references and meet her in person to gain additional insight into her personality.

Don't be surprised—and don't despair!—if by the end of the screening process, your list of candidates has dwindled by half. Remember, the whole purpose of Basic Screening is to separate the truly viable candidates from the nonstarters. The good news is that you should now have a promising list of contenders who meet all of your Musts and are ready to move forward. It's time to learn what their previous employers have to say about them in the next step of the Gold Standard hiring process: Reference Checks.

RED FLAGS IN BASIC SCREENING

- Inconsistencies between what the candidate tells you and what is on her résumé or in her online profile
- Large gaps in her work history
- If she says she worked with a family for a long time but cannot remember the names of the parents or the children
- If you Google her name and concerning information appears, or if the details she has posted on Facebook, LinkedIn, or other social networking sites do not match what she told you
- Bouncing back and forth between childcare and other jobs
- Being short, defensive, or rude

CHAPTER 5

———

Reference Checks

Can This Nanny Do Your Job?

Now that you've used the techniques in Basic Screening to refine your list of potential candidates, it's time to really start getting to know them by moving on to references checks. Reference checks are crucial to the Gold Standard hiring process because they provide you with a unique opportunity to have another employer rate the nanny as both a professional and a person and, when the check is done correctly, can give you far more insight into a nanny's true abilities, strengths, weaknesses, and personality than an interview. This is because nannies often know how to give the right answer during an interview and will tell you what you want to hear, but 99 percent of parents will be completely honest when speaking to another parent in an off-the-record situation. For this reason, you always want to do your reference checks *before* you meet the nanny in person, so that you don't waste time interviewing someone who looks good on paper but didn't actually perform well at her last job.

Unfortunately, most parents miss the chance to gain critical information at this stage of the process because they do what I call a generic reference check, in which they call up the nanny's former employer and ask the typical generic questions:

Q: **How did you like Bonnie? Did you have a good relationship?**
A: Oh yes, we loved her.

Q: **Was she ever late?**
A: No, in four years she never took a sick day.

Q: **Did she have a good work ethic?**
A: Yes, she did everything we asked. She was great with our children. We loved her so much.

And five minutes later, the perspective employer hangs up the phone with an impeccable reference and thinks, "This is the nanny for us."

But in the Gold Standard process, the real goal of a reference check is not to find out how wonderful the nanny was in her last job; it's to find out how she would fare in *yours*. So we do what I call the "Gold Targeted Check." In a Gold Targeted Check, you flip it around and ask the reference to project what the nanny would be like in *your* household. You look at your FNA and say, "I work long hours and I'm going to be leaving my infant daughter. How do you think Bonnie would handle a twelve-hour day with an infant?" Then the mother may pause and say, "Well, I'm not sure, my children were three and six when she came to work for us, so I don't know how she'd be with a newborn. When my sister came to visit with her two-month-old from California, Bonnie seemed kind of flustered by the crying." By asking more pointed, highly specific questions that relate directly to the position you're hiring for, you may learn that their seemingly perfect nanny may not be so perfect for you.

I always tell my clients that they need to have *at least one* checkable reference for any nanny they want to hire and preferably more. That said, gathering references can sometimes be a challenge because parents everywhere are busy people. It may take several calls to get the nanny's former employer to call you back, and some may never respond to you at all. If this happens, do *not* take it as a sign that the employer didn't like the nanny or that the nanny is not worth pursuing. I've had people explain to me honestly, "Listen, I have three kids and I work part-time. I can barely do what I need to do for my family, let alone help my nanny from five years ago." Sadly, for many people, helping a former nanny—even if she was the most wonderful nanny in the world—doesn't make it onto their priority list. So don't be discouraged or write the nanny off if you are unable to track down and talk to every single reference that she provides.

When deciding which family to call first, begin with the reference that is in the best position to offer insight about how the nanny will fare in your particular job. In general, the most helpful references will be the ones where the job was most similar to yours. For example, if you have two children under the age of four, you should begin with the reference who also had nanny care for two children of similar ages. This does *not* mean that you should not check the other references that a nanny provides or that a reference for which the situation was different will not be helpful; it is merely a good place to start.

Your List of Questions: What Are You Going to Ask?

The key to a successful Gold Targeted Check is asking the right questions in the right order. This is an area where my therapist skills really come into play because reference checks, along with interviews, are all about asking questions to try to gain the most accurate picture possible of each candidate and who they really are. Good questions will allow for fact-finding and drawing out information that pertains to your particular situation; bad questions will waste time and tell you more about the reference and his or her own personal likes and dislikes than they will about the nanny. So before you pick up the phone and start making your calls, you want to use your FNA to come up with a list of questions that will elicit the specific insights you need to know about whether a nanny is right for you.

In therapy, we use what are called open-ended questions, such as those beginning with *how* or *why*, because they require a more detailed answer or explanation rather than just a simple yes or no. Remember, you are trying to fill in the pieces of your nanny puzzle, and yes or no (or what we call closed-ended) questions won't uncover the kind of details that you need to get the true measure of a nanny and her abilities. For instance, take the following two examples:

REFERENCE CHECK USING CLOSED-ENDED QUESTIONS

Q: **Did you like Edna as a nanny?**
A: Yes, we loved her. [But you and the reference may be different, so you may not like what she liked.]

Q: **Did she perform her duties well?**
A: Yes, always. [But you may have different standards, and your duties may be completely different as well.]

Q: **Did your children like her?**
A: Yes, very much. [But your children may be very different.]

REFERENCE CHECK USING OPEN-ENDED QUESTIONS

Q: **How would you describe Edna?**
A: Edna was an older woman who provided a stable, calm presence for our children.

Q: **Can you tell me specifically what she did in
your home?**

A: She really focused on taking care of the house, but she also took
care of the children. She prepared their meals, did their laundry,
and kept their rooms clean. She would check in from time to time
to make sure their homework was being done.

Q: **We have two young children at home who require a
great deal of energy. Do you think Edna could keep
up with a two- and three-year-old?**

A: No, I really do not think she would be suited to children of that
age. She was kind, dependable, trustworthy, and very loving, but
I do not think she would have the emotional or physical stamina
for younger children.

As you can see, the open-ended questions reveal a much different
picture of the candidate. I always advise my clients to ask open-ended
questions whenever possible because doing so will force the reference
to elaborate and share concrete examples from her experience with the
nanny.

How to Structure a Reference Check

A Gold Targeted Check has three main parts:

1. Confirm the details of the nanny's previous job to make sure that
   the nanny and reference are legit. Ask about general traits and
   characteristics to fill in the picture of who this nanny is.
2. See if the nanny can match your Musts.
3. Run scenarios and ask the reference to project how the nanny
   would fare in those scenarios.

The check is structured in order of importance, beginning with the questions that *only* a reference can answer. For example, only a past employer can verify that the information the nanny gave you about her work history is correct. Part 1 also contains key questions intended to test the legitimacy of the reference because if a reference isn't real, there's no point in continuing on. Therefore, if you are speaking with a reference who is pressed for time or who seems impatient and reluctant to answer a lot of questions, you should focus on Part 1 because it is designed to quickly give you the most critical information. Most of the questions in Parts 2 and 3 can be answered, at least to some degree, during the interview and trials; for example, you can set up scenarios to test the nanny's ability to follow directions or assess how she handles a toddler when she is in your home for a dry run.

Now let's take a closer look at each part of the check and at how to come up with your list of questions for each one.

PART 1: CONFIRM THE DETAILS OF THE NANNY'S PREVIOUS JOB, AND ASK ABOUT HER GENERAL PERFORMANCE

The first part of the call asks the reference to confirm the information that the nanny gave you during Basic Screening. You should start by asking the reference to review the exact parameters of the nanny's previous job—the dates the nanny worked there, the number of the children and their ages, the duties, and the starting and ending salary—to see if what she says matches what the nanny told you. Then, asking open-ended questions, you want to get some insight into the nanny's overall job performance, just in case the call gets cut short. What were the nanny's strengths and weaknesses? Why did the nanny leave and was she in good standing when she left? Most important, you want to ask, "Was there ever a time when the candidate was dishonest?" and "Were there any times when you questioned the nanny's judgment?" Asking about a nanny's judgment is a catchall question that can reveal all sorts of things that don't fall into any childcare-related category, from an abusive boyfriend behind the scenes to a problem with credit card debt. Together, these questions provide an immediate read on whether the nanny has been truthful about her work history and experience and her character overall.

Unfortunately, some nannies do list fake references and some will even list a personal friend rather than an actual employer, so this part of the check is also designed to trip up and expose any fakes. Asking for nitty-gritty details such as, "What time did the nanny start in the morning?" along with specifics about her duties, salary, and the exact dates that she worked in the household will usually cause a fake reference to stumble. Similarly, asking "How did you find your nanny?"— a very easy and straightforward question for any parent—will often stump a person who is lying. If the reference is fumbling or can't provide any specifics or something just doesn't seem right, trust your gut and end the call. Obviously, any nanny who lists a fake reference should be taken out of consideration.

PART 2: SEE IF THE NANNY CAN MATCH YOUR MUSTS

Once you've established the basics of how a nanny fared at her previous job, it's time to focus on *your* nanny position and what you need. For this stage of the call, you want to take your list of physical and emotional Musts from your FNA and describe for the reference exactly what your job entails. You are asking the reference, based on her own experience with the candidate, to give an opinion on whether the nanny is up for the job and whether or not she could handle the various responsibilities that pertain to your needs as a parent and the developmental needs of your child. This is also the time to share your

---

HOW TO SPOT A FAKE REFERENCE

Here are some easy ways to determine up front whether or not a reference is the real deal:

- **Does the reference have the same ethnic accent as the nanny?** If so, it can be a tip-off that you are probably not talking to a real family or employer. Sometimes nannies who are new to this country will work for a friend without actually getting paid, so if you encounter this, you want to press the reference: "Did you pay her money? How much money? And can you tell me what time she started and what she did during the day?" Usually, when faced with these questions, a fake reference will become evasive or cop to the truth.
- **Ask, "How did this candidate come to work for you?"** A parent will answer this question readily, but a fake reference will almost always be caught off guard and will have to make up a story on the fly. If they say, "Through a friend," ask, "Which friend?" If they can't answer or stumble, the reference is probably not real.
- **Delve into details.** If the reference cannot remember start dates or the nanny's exact hours or her salary or what she did all day long with the children or how many years she was with the family, the reference is most likely bogus.
- **Ask for examples.** A real parent will be able to give you plenty of examples of both the good and the bad about their former nanny. If they can't, they are either lying about the nanny—maybe she wasn't as good or as incompetent as they say she was—or they are not a real reference.

Deal-Breakers and make sure that the reference doesn't feel they are going to be a problem.

PART 3: RUN SCENARIOS

In the last part of the check, have the reference confirm your vision by giving her specific scenarios based on your FNA and asking her to project how the nanny would handle them. For example, you might describe your worst-day scenario and then ask the reference how she thinks the nanny would fare. This is a perfect time to delve into any aspects of the job that may make your nanny position challenging—such as your highly sensitive child or your two wild preschool boys. To prepare for this part of the check, review your FNA and come up with a few scenarios that are unique to your family and household. You will be able to use these scenarios again with the nanny herself when it's time to do the interview.

Sample Reference Questions

QUESTIONS FOR PART 1 (ESSENTIAL INFORMATION)

Introduction: "To start, I'd just like to ask you some questions to confirm what Jennifer told me about her time working for you."

- How did Jennifer come to work for you initially?
- How long did she work for you? Can you verify the exact dates?
- Was the position live-in or live-out?
- Can you please tell me the exact working days and hours?
- How many children did Jennifer care for and what were their ages when she started?
- What were her exact duties?

- Do you mind if I ask you what you paid her? How did that compare to her salary when she first started?
- Why is Jennifer no longer with you? If she left voluntarily, did she give you notice?
- Can you please describe her greatest strengths as a nanny?
- What areas were weaknesses or areas that needed improvement?
- Was there ever a time when Jennifer was dishonest or showed poor judgment?
- Did her home life ever affect her work performance?

QUESTIONS FOR PART 2 (YOUR MUSTS)

Introduction: "Can I tell you about my job and what I'm looking for in a nanny? I'd like to know if, based on your experience with Jennifer, you think that she is a good fit for the position."

Physical "Musts":

- "Our nanny position is live-in. If your position was also live-in, can you tell me how it worked? Did she ever come home late at night and disturb the family? How was she about respecting your family's privacy?"
- "I'm at home part-time, so I am looking for a partner nanny and need someone who can split the responsibilities fifty–fifty. Do you think she could work with me as a partner and also run the show when I am gone? Do you think her personality would be suited to switching from assistant to boss?"
- "My husband and I both work late some nights so we need a nanny who is flexible. Can you tell me how the candidate was in regard to schedule changes?"
- "We are going to need our nanny to drive our children to school and activities. Can you tell me about the candidate's use of your car and if there were any issues?"

Emotional "Musts":

- "I'm a new mom, and I don't want a nanny who is bossy, but I do want someone who can provide some guidance around sleep training and potty training. Was Jennifer helpful in this way with your family? And if so, how?"
- "As mentioned, our child is _____ years old. How do you think Jennifer would be handling the developmental needs of:

  - Infant (0–1), such as bottle feeding, handling colic, soothing the baby, and establishing schedules? Does she have a warm, loving, and very positive attitude?
  - Toddler (1–3), such as having the physical energy to run after them and keep them safe or the emotional energy and patience to play with them and handle tantrums?
  - Preschooler (3–5), such as learning and writing letters and numbers, reading books, doing arts and crafts, and teaching manners? Do you think she would know how to encourage them and when to help them versus let them do things on their own?
  - School age (5–9), such as giving social support around trouble with friends or teachers, and helping with homework or other school activities?
  - Tween/teen (10–18), such as maintaining a positive relationship with them, even if they may want to break the rules and not do what they are asked?"

Deal-Breakers:

- "I am a stickler about being punctual. Can you tell me how Jennifer did with being on time? Was she ever late, and if so, how did she handle it?"
- "I really do not want a lot of cell phone or TV use. Do you think

she would adhere to these rules? What would she use instead of TV to keep the kids busy?"

QUESTIONS FOR PART 3 (SAMPLE SCENARIOS)

Introduction: "Can I describe a couple of scenarios that might happen in our household and have you tell me how you think Jennifer would respond?"

- "How do you think she would react if I said, "I read an article about letting the baby sleep this way (or play this way) and I would like you to try it with my baby"? How did Jennifer do with receiving redirection or constructive criticism from you?"
- "Our son is very fussy about his bath and sometimes bath time requires a lot of patience. If the nanny can't keep him happy and distracted, bath time can end in a total meltdown. How do you think Jennifer would manage this scenario and do you think she would have the creativity and patience to get through it?"

How to Make the Call

Calling references can often feel like selling newspapers. Some parents will give you all the time in the world, while others won't even pick up the phone. So what should you do?

The Gold Standard strategy is to keep your initial call short and sweet. You want to call up the person, quickly explain who you are and why you're calling, and then offer another time or way to get the information. You want to be extremely respectful and grateful for their time, and appeal to them as a fellow parent. The following script grew out of my own experience checking references, and my recruiters have used it with great success. Here's how it works:

1. **Identify yourself and your purpose quickly:** "Hello, my name is Tammy Gold, and I'm calling about your former nanny, Jennifer. We're considering hiring her as a nanny for our children, and I was wondering if you had a few minutes to answer some questions?"

2. **Give them the option to give the reference another time:** "I'm sure you're very busy. Would you like to speak now, or would you like to speak at another time? I could also send you the questions via email if that's easier."

3. **Thank them:** "Thank you so much, and I'm sure that Jennifer also really appreciates your taking the time to answer these questions."

4. **Appeal to them as a fellow parent:** "And parent to parent, I really appreciate it, because we really like Jennifer and hearing about your experience with her, and getting your perspective will be enormously helpful for us in making this decision. Thank you again for taking the time."

During the Call

While you're on the call with a reference, take as many notes as you can and ask for clarification when you need it. Here are some additional tips for gathering information both efficiently and effectively:

- **Don't get pulled into a lot of stories about them.** Sometimes a reference will get caught up in sharing memories about the nanny or start waxing philosophical about her other nanny experiences. If this happens, feel free to cut her off and gently direct her back to information that is more relevant to you. Remember, her personal experiences are not as important as the insights she can give you about the nanny in *your* job.

- **If the reference is negative, try to figure out why.** Anything negative is helpful only if the reference can articulate *why* she felt that way. If the reference says, "Oh, she just rubbed me the wrong way," be sure to ask, "*Why* did she rub you the wrong way? *What* exactly did she do that bothered you?" If the reference can't give you specific examples and anecdotes, don't place too much stock in what she says.
- **Beware of moms with ulterior motives.** Just as you need to play detective and try to figure out who the nanny is, you also want to use your judgment about the reference. Don't assume that a reference is correct and don't take everything she says on blind faith. Sometimes parents, especially if the nanny quit, will have their own issues or an ax to grind that has nothing to do with the true abilities of a nanny.

Reference Recap: Assessing What You've Learned

After you've completed your call, you should review your notes and take stock of what you've learned. If the reference is positive and enthusiastic overall, your decision to move forward with the candidate will be easy. But not all references will be glowing. What should you do if the reference reveals flaws?

- **Assess the source.** How did you feel about the reference when you spoke to her? Could it be that the mom was difficult or the family was hard to work for? If the mom had ridiculously high expectations and you have a more reasonable, rational approach, then the nanny may be just fine.
- **Decide if the negatives are relevant to your job.** If the nanny and the mom clashed and battled over territory because they were in the

house together all day long, but you're going to be at work all day, then this particular problem doesn't relate to you.

- **Talk to other references.** If a nanny has multiple references, you should talk to them specifically about the issue to see if it was ever a concern. If not, it may have been situation specific—for example, maybe she was often late to work at that one particular job because it was a more challenging commute.

- **Can you test the concern in the interview or trial?** For example, if the mom noted that the nanny was not always the best at being proactive, present the nanny with the issue during the interview: "We spoke to Linda and she said wonderful things. Her one area of concern was around being proactive. We really need someone who can be proactive and take charge because we are both at work all day. Is this something you can do?" The nanny may be able to explain away the concern: "It was hard to be proactive, because I was watching three kids and cleaning the whole house top to bottom every week—there was no time to work ahead or do anything else." Or she may become defensive, which is not a good sign. You can also test for proactivity during a trial, by seeing if she starts folding the big pile of laundry on the bed or picking up the toys and putting them away.

- **If you need more info, call the reference back.** If something was unclear or is still troubling you, call the reference back or email her and say, "Thank you so much for your time, it was tremendously helpful talking to you, and parent to parent, I appreciate it so much. There was something you mentioned about an issue with camp; would you mind telling me more about that?"

After you've completed your reference checks, you should be able to narrow down your pool of candidates even more and identify a few top choices. In the next step, you'll move on to finally meet the nannies face to face in the next stage of the Gold Standard process: Interviews.

WHAT IF A NANNY HAS NO REFERENCES?

A nanny who has recently arrived in the United States or a young person who is looking to be a nanny for the first time may not have references from a previous family that you can check. If she has no past childcare experience, ask for any type of job reference so that you can find out how she was as an employee. If she has no references of any kind, but you really like her and she meets all of the Musts from your FNA, you can do an interview and extra-long trials so that you can spend a lot of time with her and get to know her as much as possible. You should also do a very thorough background check to verify that she has no criminal history and that the rest of the information she has given you is real.

CHAPTER 6

———•———

Interviews

Meet the Candidates and
Ask Them to Match Your Story

At last, it's time to meet your top candidates face to face. The good news is that because you've already done your screening and your reference checks, the nannies who you meet in person are the ones who have the greatest chance of actually being right for your job. Interviews are a vital part of the Gold Standard hiring process because they give you the opportunity to fill in additional details about the candidate and to pose questions designed to reveal how she would care for your children and fit in with your household. You've already filled in a lot of the pieces of your nanny puzzle by doing Basic Screening and Reference Checks; now it's finally time to fill in the missing piece about how you and the nanny interact.

However, as I've said many times before, the nanny world is the Wild West where 1 + 1 doesn't always equal 2. That's why I always tell my clients that interviews in the nanny world can mean absolutely nothing. I've seen nannies who were amazing and polished during the interview be completely terrible during the trial, and I've seen nannies who struck the parents as being too boring or quiet during the interview come to life in the most wonderful way when interacting with children. My own nanny, Maria, barely said two words during our interview, but she came highly recommended by all of her past employers, and when I saw her in action, I knew that she was the perfect nanny for us. The truth is that many nannies are not great interviewers because they are not used to a setting that's more typical of the professional world: They're nervous and there may be language issues (or even cultural or class-related issues) that make easy communication difficult or uncomfortable.

But, and this is one of the things I try hardest to impress upon parents: *A nanny doesn't have to be great in an interview to be an incredible nanny.* She doesn't have to be able to sit for two hours while people fire very difficult questions at her. She has to love children, and she has to be good at what she does. So your goal with the interview is *not* to figure out

> A nanny doesn't have to be great in an interview to be an incredible nanny.

if you and the nanny can get along happily for the next ten years or to grill her on obscure details of child development. Instead, you want to ask questions that will help you further understand her and to as-

SHOULD YOUR CHILDREN BE PRESENT DURING AN INTERVIEW?

I do not think it is necessary for children to be involved in interviews. Children can be distracting, and this is the time for you and the nanny to speak and connect. Don't use the interview to assess how the nanny is with your child; that's what the trial is for.

sess the basics: Did she arrive on time? Is she neatly dressed? Does she say anything that seems abnormal or off? She may answer your questions eloquently, or she may not—but all you need to decide is whether she seems generally pleasant and competent and if she meets enough of your Musts to have her come to your house and do a trial.

Setting Up Interviews

Some parents like to tackle all of their interviews in a single day, while others prefer to do one at a time, so you should do whatever feels right and least stressful for you. Begin with your top candidates and call or email them to arrange a time to meet. I tell parents to aim for thirty minutes per interview, but to schedule an hour for each candidate in case you need extra time.

Once you finalize a time for the interview, you should:

- Explain that you are going to be doing interviews first, followed by paid trials if the interview goes well. This way the nanny knows what to expect.
- Ask her to bring along her working status papers and driver's license so that you can ask her any questions about them during the interview and have the information on hand for background checks. You should also ask her to bring a current utility or credit card bill in her name to verify her present address. You can use your smartphone to take a photo of the front and back of each document or use a home scanner to make a copy.
- Arrange to meet at a relaxed location. You want to keep the interview as informal as possible for all parties so that the nanny feels comfortable opening up. If you'd rather not invite candidates into your home just yet, try a neutral location such as a coffee shop.

How to Structure an Interview

A Gold Standard interview has three parts. First, you start by telling your story, reviewing the details of the position, and reiterating what you are looking for in a nanny. Then, you ask the candidate to match her experience to your story, so that you can assess the degree of fit. Finally, you finish up with some additional personal questions to get a clearer sense of who the nanny is as an individual and professionally. Be prepared to take notes throughout the conversation, so that you can review what you've learned and assess the pros and cons after you're done.

PART 1: TELL YOUR STORY

Even though you already described your job and talked to the nanny about her credentials during Basic Screening, you want to go over your lists of Musts, Pluses, and Deal-Breakers from your FNA one more time during the interview, so the nanny can hear them again and respond face to face. If you've had other nannies or childcare providers, you also want to explain what has worked and not worked well for you in the past so that the candidate has a very clear sense of what you want. You should also mention any preemployment tests that you would like her to do, for example, a driving test or physical health exam. Then, you want to present the scenarios that you came up with based on your FNA (you can use the same ones you used during Reference Checks) about your worst day and other common situations in your household.

Keep in mind that this is the time for you to be as open and honest as possible about every single aspect of your job—the positive aspects as well as the challenging ones—and about what you want (and don't want) in a caregiver. You should also make a point of telling the nanny that you would like her to be open and honest as well and that it will be helpful to hear about her likes and dislikes and about how she works best so that together you can decide if you're a match.

Script and Sample Questions for Part 1

Introduction: "Barbara, I know that we already talked about the requirements and duties for our position, but we'd like to go over them again so that we can answer any questions you may have. I'd also like to tell you about the kind of partnership we hope to have and about what has worked well and not worked well for us with our past nannies. We really want you to answer honestly, and to tell us about how you work, and your likes and dislikes when working with families, because all of this will help us to get to know you and figure out if we're a fit."

1. **Reconfirm that the candidate meets your basic requirements:** "Just to confirm, Barbara, you can work Monday through Friday from 7 a.m. to 7 p.m. and have the flexibility to stay one night a week, correct?"

2. **Explain any preemployment requirements and see how the nanny feels:** "For our top candidates, we will be doing a full background check, a drug test, and a physical exam, which we will pay for. Is this OK with you, and may I take pictures of your documents?"

3. **Review any additional Musts, Pluses, and Deal-Breakers:** "I am a full-time mom, and I love being hands-on with my daughters. While I am with the kids, I need someone to do cooking, cleaning, and housekeeping. Then, when I am out with one of the girls, you would play games and read to the other. Are you OK with this type of arrangement? Also, we feel very strongly that our nanny use a cell phone only during naptime or in an emergency. Is this something that you can agree to?"

4. **Talk about what has worked and not worked well with past caregivers:** "Our baby nurse sometimes had issues with being late, and after I return to work, our nanny cannot be late because my job starts early."

5. **Tell her about the hardest part of the job:** "It can be very difficult on days when our baby is not feeling good and is crying. Usually that's the day that our toddler wants additional attention— probably because she is watching us give the baby extra care. We need someone who can manage both infant and toddler needs."

6. **Pose additional scenarios and ask how the nanny would handle them:** "Yesterday my baby would not stop crying. How would you handle this?"

PART 2: ASK THE NANNY TO MATCH YOUR STORY

This part of the interview allows the nanny to take the lead and share the experiences she feels would make her right for your particular job. You can begin by asking the nanny very broadly to explain why she feels that she is a good fit and then shift to specific questions based on your physical and emotional Musts and FNA if necessary to prompt her.

Script and Sample Questions for Part 2

Introduction: "Now that we have told you what we are looking for, can you tell us about any experiences in your professional or personal life that would make you a good fit for this position?"

1. **Ask her to tell you about her duties at each of her previous jobs:** "What was your typical day with the Jones family? Can you tell me what you did from the time you started in the morning until you finished in the evening?"

2. Pose specific questions based on your physical and emotional Musts. You should use these questions to cover any topics that the nanny did not address when describing her duties at her previous jobs. For example:

- "As we mentioned, we are looking for a nanny who can take complete charge of our children and our household while we are at work sixty hours a week. Can you tell me about a time when you did this for a previous family? Were you comfortable in that kind of director's role?"
- "As we said, we need a nanny who can travel with us approximately four times a year. Can you tell me about any travel you've done in the past with another family?"
- "As we said, our child is ____ years old. Can you tell me about any experience you have with:

  - Infant (0–1), such as helping to soothe a baby, sleep training, or putting a baby on a schedule?
  - Toddler (1–3), such as toilet training, dealing with tantrums? How did you handle keeping them safe?
  - Preschooler (3–5), such as how did you teach letters and numbers, and how to share?
  - School age (5–9), such as have you ever helped with homework or helped a child feel better after not doing well at a sports game?
  - Tween/teen (10–18), such as have you ever had to work through a situation in which a teen lied to you, or comforted a teen after a breakup?"

PART 3: PERSONAL QUESTIONS

Now that you've covered all the specifics related to your job, you want to try to get to know the nanny as a person as much as possible. This last part of the interview allows you to try to fill in any remaining gaps in her timeline. Ideally, you want this part of the interview to feel like a friendly, casual, get-to-know-you conversation.

Script and Sample Questions for Part 3

Introduction: "Now, if it's OK, we'd like to learn a little bit more about you personally, and about how you came to be a nanny."

1. **Ask her to tell you about her life up until now:** "Everyone has a special story that makes her unique, so I'm wondering if you can tell me yours. I'll tell you mine first: My name is Sandra and I was born in Ontario, Canada, in 1970. I lived with my parents and my two sisters, then I went to college and studied economics. I moved to America in 2001 and went to work for a bank. I met my husband, Charles, and we got married in 2007 and had twin girls in 2010. In 2012, I went to work for another firm, and then we

---

GETTING PERSONAL: WHERE DO YOU DRAW THE LINE?

When it comes to hiring someone to care for your children, you have every right to ask as many questions as necessary to feel confident about whom you hire. While federal and state discrimination laws make it illegal to ask about someone's age, race, national origin, religion, family, marital status, parental status, sexual orientation, or personal life during a job interview, these laws do *not* apply to employers who employ fewer than fifteen people. If there is something you need to know but are hesitant to ask, you can broach the topic this way: "I know that some of these questions may seem personal, but since you will be coming into our home and will be very intimately involved with our family, we really want to get to know you as much as possible. Can you tell me...?"

---

bought this house a year ago, and now I balance part-time work with running after my two little ladies. That's my story, can you share yours?"

2. **If there are gaps in her story, probe about her background and family life,** by asking questions such as these:

   "Where were you born?"

   "When and why did you come to the United States?"

   "Where do you currently live? Do you live alone?"

   "Who watches your children when you go to work?"

   "What are your hobbies?"

3. **Ask her about being a nanny:**

   "What made you want to be a nanny?"

   "What is the best part of being a nanny?"

   "What is the hardest part of being a nanny?"

   "What are you looking for in a new family? What is most important to you?"

   "What jobs did you hold before being a nanny? How did you get from being a _____ to nannying? Do you plan on returning to your earlier career? If so, when?"

4. **Ask her about each of her previous nanny jobs:** "What was the best aspect of working for the Jones family and why? What was the most difficult aspect of working for them and why?"

Tips for a Successful Interview

While you are conducting the interview, listen closely to how the nanny responds to your questions, and observe her mannerisms and general demeanor. Here are some things to keep in mind throughout the conversation:

- **How you treat the nanny matters.** Good nannies will be sizing you up as well, so start the interview off right by greeting the nanny warmly and/or welcoming her into your home, just as you would any other guest.
- **A nanny's strong suit is interacting with children, not necessarily interviewing with adults.** Sometimes a nanny is not as polished, professional, or well spoken as the parents, but this does not necessarily reflect how she will be as a caregiver. So keep an open mind, and try not to judge the nanny by the same standards you would use when interviewing someone in your profession.
- **Nannies are trying to make you like them.** Nannies want to impress you, so they may overcompensate by being too deferential, overly eager, or trying too hard to cozy up to you or your children. Often they will act the way they believe you want them to based on their experience with other employers. You can help her to feel comfortable and show her true personality by setting a relaxed tone.
- **Don't pressure yourself to know if a candidate is The One.** There is no way to know if you have found the perfect caregiver during an interview, so don't push yourself to decide because this stress will only cloud the process. Take the pressure off and use this meeting to simply decide if the candidate is worth meeting again for a trial.
- **If you feel uncomfortable, end the interview.** There is no rule that you need to do a complete interview with every candidate. If at any point during the interview you feel uncomfortable or know without question that this is not the right nanny—for example, if she is rude, or says something to offend you—end the interview. You can simply say, "Thank you for your time; we will be in touch about any next steps."
- **Remember, no one is perfect.** Just as you are not perfect, there will be pros and cons to every candidate. Don't look for perfection; instead, look for a nanny who has more and stronger pros than cons.

INTERVIEWS: WHAT YOUR NANNY IS THINKING

I can't tell you how many calls I've received from nannies after interviews that began like this: "Tammy, thank you so much for sending me to the Smith family, but I would like to withdraw my application."

Some families mistakenly think they hold all the power during an interview, but that is not the case. Good nannies will have no trouble finding a good job, so they are interviewing you just as much as you are interviewing them. There have been many times when I sent an incredible nanny to a family for an interview, and the parents blew it! Here are some of the reasons the nannies gave:

"The mom was so rude. She did not smile when she opened the door, and she immediately looked me up and down. She made me wash my hands and then scolded me because I did not turn off the sink correctly. She seemed annoyed the whole time, and there is no way that I would ever be able to go to that house every morning."   —Jeanette, Atlanta, GA

"The parents were so anxious and stressed. The house was in total chaos, the kids were fighting, the baby was walking around with no diaper on, and the sink was full of dirty dishes. It just seemed like the job would be totally overwhelming."
—Naomi, McLean, VA

"They fired questions at me for an hour, really difficult questions that I did not even understand sometimes. They made me feel stupid because I did not know the difference between Waldorf and Montessori learning systems. I have been a nanny for twenty-two years, and I know that I am wonderful at caring for children. I may not have the highest education, but I know how to handle kids."   —Sonya, Los Angeles, CA

Here are some of the questions that will be running through the nanny's mind during the interview:

• Are the family's needs realistic or are they too demanding?
• Is the family rigid and unfriendly or relaxed and welcoming?
• Are they treating the current nanny well or are they treating her poorly?
• Does the house seem in control and could I keep things in order?
• Could I be happy here for a long time and excited to come to work?

Remember that even though you are the employer, you should treat your nanny candidates with professional kindness and respect because if you end up choosing them, you want the feeling to be mutual.

Interview Recap: Assessing What You've Learned

After you meet with each candidate, write down your general impressions and make a list of the pros and cons. If you are not sure about your feelings, use the following questions to prompt you:

• Was the candidate on time for the interview? If not, how did she handle it?
• Did she come across as warm, loving, and friendly?
• Did you feel comfortable speaking with the candidate and feel like she was answering your questions honestly?
• Did she talk about how she enjoys working with children? Could you see in her face that she really meant it?

- Did she communicate well and were you comfortable with her language skills?
- Did she seem open to your questions? Did she answer appropriately?
- Did she have a positive and flexible attitude when you discussed the duties and requirements of the job with her?
- Was she receptive to your likes and dislikes, and willing to do things your way?
- Can you see yourself speaking frankly with this candidate without having to worry about her reaction?
- Did she seem like she was physically in good health and able to keep up with your children?
- Did she seem more focused on the pay and benefits than in the actual job or overly focused on her needs rather than yours?
- Did you experience any red flags or gut feelings that made you feel uncomfortable, such as a gruff response or extreme emotion that did not seem to fit the situation?

What to Do About Cons

As mentioned previously, every nanny is going to have cons, but some negatives may not automatically mean that you have to eliminate the candidate. If you have any concerns, try to divide them into two groups:

Fixable cons: These are the things that you did not like, but that might be fixable with teaching and training, such as a different approach to discipline, the wrong way to settle a baby ("I would never give my child a bath to stop her crying"), or what you consider to be an unhealthy way of eating ("I really didn't like what she said about snacks; I would never feed my kids that stuff!").

Personality-based cons: Negatives that can probably *not* be fixed, such as a gruff, bossy personality; a loud way of speaking that annoys you; or a rigid view that is the opposite of yours.

If a candidate has fixable cons, and you liked her personality and felt that she was open to direction, you can test the fixable con during the trial. For example: "I really didn't like what she said about calming babies, but in the trial, I will show her how we settle Gabe and see if she is able and willing to use our techniques."

Moving Forward

After the interview, it's time to decide if you would like to move forward and invite the nanny into your home to meet your children and do a trial. In general, I believe that if a nanny meets your Musts, has great references, seems pleasant and kind, and gives good answers during the interview, you should arrange to bring her into your home for a paid trial. Even if you like her but don't love her after the interview, it's almost always worth it to see her on the job and with your children because you may very well come to see the nanny and what she brings to the table in a whole new light.

Now it's time to move on to the part of your search where everything comes together: the Trials.

CHAPTER 7

———

Trials

Observe Your Top Candidates in Action

In the Gold Standard process, trials are mandatory because, in my experience, they are the *only* way that you can know for certain that a particular nanny is right for your job. Plenty of nannies will assure you, "Yes, I can do that," during Basic Screening or an Interview, but a trial gives you a chance to assess firsthand whether she can walk the walk as well as talk the talk. Is she, as she said, proactive? Is she comfortable with newborns? Can she actually handle a twelve-hour day with a toddler? And just as important, is this someone who you can envision having in your home every day helping you raise your child?

Some parents feel that trials are unnecessary and, if they're rushed, will come up with any excuse they can to avoid them. But trust me when I tell you that there is *no way* to glean how a nanny will fare in your job or how the chemistry will be until you've actually worked alongside her and seen her in action with your children. I always insist that my clients do two full-day trials if possible, so that the nanny can experience an actual day on the job, including any commute. This is because the number one reason that nannies quit is because the commute is too hard on top of a long day, and the number two reason is that the hours and duties of the job prove to be too much. Full-day trials give you a chance to show all your cards so that there are no surprises after the nanny starts.

I strongly recommend doing two full-days rather than one because that's how long it generally takes to get an accurate sense of a nanny's true skills and personality. On the first day of the trial everyone is nervous, and everything—from the layout of your house to your daily routines—will be unfamiliar to her. By day two, the comfort level is greater, and you can see how well she employs what she learned on day one. Furthermore, anyone can give their best for a couple of hours, but not everyone can be at the top of their game for an entire day. If the nanny seems to lose motivation as the day goes on, or if she starts to become impatient with your child as she gets

---

WHAT IF YOU CAN'T DO TWO FULL DAYS?

If you absolutely can't manage two full-day trials due to work, I recommend doing two separate half-day trials rather than one full day. The first one should be in the morning, so that the nanny can experience the first half of a typical day, including her morning commute. The second one should be in the afternoon/evening so she can experience any end-of-day duties such as dinner and bath time along with the commute home afterward. This way, the nanny gets a clear sense of every piece of your daily routine, and you still get the chance to assess her progress and any changes between day one and day two. If you are working and can't do trials during the week, you can always do them for a few hours at night or on the weekends.

tired, it's much better to find out these things now so that you don't make a mistake in whom you hire.

Trials also give you an opportunity to test the pros and cons for each candidate that came up during your reference checks and interviews. To do this, you purposefully create a scenario to either test or confirm the nanny's abilities in an area that's important to you. For example, if the nanny was a little bit late to the interview and you are worried about punctuality, for the trial, you can give her hard-and-fast times to arrive in the morning, to be home after she takes the kids to the park, and to have dinner on the table. By doing this, you will be able to see if she can follow basic instructions regarding time and manage to stick to a daily schedule.

Trials are always paid, especially because some nannies will need to take time off from another job to do them. You should expect to pay the average hourly rate for your market and to pay the nanny at

PREGNANCY TRIALS: WHAT TO DO WHEN THERE ARE NO KIDS

Even if you and your partner are expecting, you can still have a productive trial before the baby comes. I've had clients who borrowed their nieces and nephews or the child of a friend to test the nanny's caregiving skills and observe how she interacted with the children. In other cases, we simply focused on the parent–nanny match and had the nanny come to help the mom set up the nursery and do additional work around the house. The mom was still able to assess the nanny as an employee—Did she follow directions? Was she easy to correct and redirect?—and get a sense of whether their communication and interaction would be comfortable.

the end of the shift, regardless of whether or not you liked her. I recommend that you trial *at least* two candidates so that you have a good point of comparison, but there is no rule that says you can't trial every candidate who crosses your path. You can either schedule each candidate for two days back to back, or do a one-day trial with each to start and then bring your top choices back for a second day. Trialing multiple candidates is always a good idea because the differences between them will be illuminating, and it's also good to have a runner-up in case your first-choice nanny drops out at the last minute. No matter how much time you invest in a particular candidate, a nanny is almost always weighing other job options besides yours.

> When we hired our first nanny, I was reluctant to do trials. No one else I knew had done them, and I was so exhausted from not sleeping that I honestly didn't want to take the time. But what I totally underestimated was just how much my opinion of someone could change after seeing them in my house, doing the job. I was convinced that we were going to hire the first woman we trialed, because she had great references and really impressed us in the interview. But she turned out to have some weird—and very firm—ideas about how to do things, such as rinsing the baby's bottom off in the sink whenever she changed a diaper. As a first-time mom, I didn't have the confidence to tell her no, and every time she did this, my six-week-old son peed all over the bathroom and I had to clean it up. I was so relieved when she left that I almost considered quitting my job just so I wouldn't have to hire a nanny at all. Fortunately, we stuck with it and did more trials, and ultimately found someone who we really love.
>
> —LAUREN, LOS ANGELES, CA

How to Structure a Trial

A trial should mirror an actual day on the job as much as possible, so that you can see how the nanny responds to a variety of situations and can give her a realistic sense of what the job entails. Throughout the trials, you want to share as much information about your household and give her as much direction as possible. Don't be afraid to overwhelm the nanny because you want only the strongest candidates to survive!

DAY ONE

Day one of the trial is all about providing the nanny with lots of guidance and information, on everything from where you keep the sippy cups to what kinds of vegetables your children will eat to how to calm your son during a tantrum. You should create a written schedule for the day along with a list of any additional to-dos. Writing them down—as opposed to just telling the nanny—is important because she will be able to refer to your instructions as she goes to make sure she is getting everything done. For example:

SCHEDULE

- **8:00 a.m.:** Dress Lily and Max in the clothes that are on the bed and bring them to the kitchen.
- **8:30 a.m.:** Prepare a simple breakfast (cereal, eggs, or waffles) and then feed the children and clear the dishes. If time permits, place the dishes in the dishwasher. If not, handle the dishes during naptime.
- **9:00 a.m.:** Put Lily in the stroller and walk to school.
- **9:30 a.m.:** After dropping Max off at school, return home and

play with Lily (flash cards, puppets, blocks) or read books for thirty minutes.

• **10:00 a.m.:** Lily goes down for her first nap. Lily's nap routine: Read her a book and rock her in the rocking chair, then place her in the crib and turn on her mobile. Please place her in the crib when she is awake but sleepy—she will cry for a few minutes, sometimes longer, but this is OK because we are sleep training her.

TO-DO LIST

• Take the recycling to the recycle bin in the garage
• Empty the diaper pail before you go home

On the Day of the Trial

Once the nanny arrives, you should start out by giving her a complete physical and emotional orientation of your home. A physical orientation refers to the physical aspects of your home (the layout, the entrances, where things are kept) as well as any specific guidance on schedules, duties, and how you would like her to perform certain tasks. An emotional orientation helps the nanny understand your family's intrapersonal dynamics and the emotional makeup of each child. By giving her plenty of information about both the physical and emotional aspects of the job, you will be helping the nanny do her best and give you an accurate sense of her abilities.

PHYSICAL ORIENTATION

1. **Give her a complete tour of your home.** You want to point out where all of the important household items or children's supplies are kept and let the nanny know if there are any areas that are off limits.

2. **Explain where items go.** If you plan to have the nanny wash

dishes or bottles or put the laundry away, you will need to show her where these things go.

3. **Explain the schedule for the day.** Talk through the schedule and to-do list with the nanny so she knows exactly what is expected, and allow her to ask questions as you go.

4. **Discuss any specific rules that may be unique to your family.** Every family has special rules and tasks that they want done a certain way, so it is better to tell the nanny what you want up front rather than have her make a mistake. For example: "We don't like the children to sleep in dirty clothes, so please change their clothes before naps if they become dirty at mealtimes or while playing outside."

EMOTIONAL ORIENTATION

1. **Explain each child's temperament and how to approach him or her.** You want to arm the nanny with loads of information on each child, such as how the child usually acts, what the child likes, how to soothe him, and how to get him to cooperate.

2. **Explain how to engage each child.** Many children are nervous during trials and may not want to interact with the nanny right away. You can help her by suggesting ways to connect with your child.

3. **Tell her what to do if your child is being difficult.** You want to anticipate any potential struggles and arm the nanny with your approved tactics for managing the situation. For example:

   - "If Sam won't get in the stroller, you may give him a lollipop for the ride."
   - "Sometimes Sasha will not get dressed in the morning. We usually give her a choice of two outfits and she picks one, but if she throws a tantrum, you may just have to gently put the clothes on for her."

4. **Let her know what words or childcare practices are off limits in your home.** These might include rules such as:

    • "We do not say 'good girl' or 'bad girl.' We instead use 'good choice' or 'not acceptable behavior.'"
    • "Although we respect all religions, we do not want anything religious being discussed around our children."

During the Trial

After you've given the nanny her orientation, hand her the schedule for the day and your list of to-dos and let her get to work, with your oversight. As the trial progresses, try to make sure that you have a chance to test every skill that you need her to have. For example, if you want her to do cooking for the children, make sure that you let her prepare at least one meal on her own, while you stand aside and offer only basic guidance. If you need her to be proactive, leave some dirty dishes in the sink and see if she volunteers to wash them.

If the nanny makes a mistake, or goes about something the wrong way, don't hesitate to correct her. Seeing how she handles correction and redirection is one of the most important aspects of the trial. Is she open to your input? Does she listen well? Or does she bristle and say, "I've been a nanny for fifteen years, and I know how to pack a diaper bag!" No nanny should have a problem with redirection, as long as it's done in a respectful way.

Here are some additional dos and don'ts for a successful trial:

DO realize that every nanny will make mistakes. Any new job has a learning curve. Far more important than making a mistake is how she handles it and how well she learns between day one and day two.

DON'T assess the skills, assess the motivation. Most skills—such as how to comfort your toddler or prepare his sandwich in just the right way—are teachable. What you want to see from a nanny during the trial is drive, energy, and an innate willingness to please and help however she can.

DO step back. You should be present for the first few hours of the trial, but then step back and let the nanny take charge. You can be busy in the next room or working on your laptop while still keeping an ear out to see how things are going when you're not there.

DON'T assess for the child–nanny bond. It is possible that your child might take to someone immediately, but in most cases bonding between nannies and children takes time. Don't hold it against her if your child doesn't warm up.

DON'T fault the nanny for being nervous. A nanny is on an audition for your entire family, so she may be shy or even overly talkative because she is trying hard to figure out how to please you and your children. You can encourage her by being relaxed and patient and showing her what kinds of actions get the best results.

DO be appreciative. Nannies do best with lots of appreciation and support, and the more you give them, the better they will perform.

Day One Recap: Assessing What You've Learned

After you've completed day one of the trial, you should reflect on how the day went and how you feel about the nanny. The following questions are designed to prompt you:

- Was the nanny on time?
- Did you feel comfortable around her? If not, why?
- Did she understand your directions and day you planned for her?

- Was she proactive and willing to learn?
- If she made mistakes, was she willing to fix them?
- Did she have the energy to keep up with your children and your routine?
- Do you feel better about any concerns you had during the interview?
- What did the nanny do well?
- What did she not do well?

Once you have thought about the answers to these questions, you should make a list of the nanny's pros and cons. For example:

- She was wonderful with our baby, Emma. She was very warm, affectionate, and sweet and did a good job of keeping her happy and entertained.
- *But* she really struggled with our toddler, Josh. She did not know how to motivate him, and getting him dressed in the morning and bath time were total chaos.

After you've made your list, focus on the cons and, just as you did after the interview, try to determine which ones are fixable, and which are not. As discussed in Chapter 6, fixable cons are anything that can be remedied with teaching or training; non-fixable cons are anything that is personality based and thus unlikely to change.

MAKING A PLAN FOR DAY TWO

You should use the second day of the trial to test the pros and cons from day one. Specifically, you want to see if the cons are permanent or if you can eliminate them by giving the nanny further direction. To do this, take any concern that you have—for example, that she may not be good with toddlers because she had a difficult time with yours—and ask yourself, "How can I test that?" You then construct a scenario that will help you to determine whether her toddler skills can be improved with a little guidance or if she just doesn't have the stamina and creativity to handle that particular age group. You might

TRIALS: WHAT YOUR NANNY IS THINKING

Just as families have their list of what they want to see during a trial, nannies have their list too. Here is what nannies typically focus on:

1. **Warmth of the family.** In my experience, "kindness of parents" is the number one factor that nannies look for in a job, even above salary.
2. **Intensity of the home.** Nannies need to be OK with your in-home atmosphere. They will be thinking, "Is this a welcoming and relaxed home, or does it seem very strict and rigid?"
3. **Appreciation.** Nannies will be paying attention to see if you say thank you, if you are respectful, and if you show appreciation for their work.
4. **Consideration.** I can't tell you how many nannies have told me, "I knew that I didn't want to work there because not once during the entire trial did they ask me if I wanted something to drink or a bite of food." Show the nanny the same consideration that you would any other person in your home.
5. **Communication.** Nannies are thinking, "Is the communication clear and respectful or does it feel like they are angry or annoyed?" Nannies want parents to communicate with them professionally—just as you would in any other workplace.

plan for the second day this way: "I'll take charge of Emma so that the nanny can spend more time with Josh. I'll tell her what he likes to do and play and how to motivate him with treats, and then we'll see if she improves."

If your concern is a personality-based con, you want to test for that as well. For example, if the nanny became defensive when you tried to correct her, create a scenario in which you can correct her again and see how she reacts. Does she become defensive just like before? Or does she take it better now that it's the second day and she's feeling more comfortable? If her reaction is the same, you are mostly likely dealing with a permanent con that will not change, no matter what you do.

DAY TWO

On day two of the trial you continue to gather more data by giving the nanny a new schedule and to-do list designed to test your pros and cons. Before you put her to work, you should review how things went on day one and then tell her what you'd like to see on day two.

Giving the Nanny Feedback

If you want the nanny to give her best, you need to present your feedback in a way that motivates her to improve. Here's how to do it:

1. **Start with the positives.** "We loved how wonderful you were with Caitlin, and everything that you did to play with her and engage her was exactly what we are looking for."
2. **Let her know that you are hopeful this can work but that you have some concerns.** "We're looking forward to having this work out, but there are a couple of things that we noticed yesterday that

we need to work on." The nanny needs to believe that if she can change the negatives, she still has a shot at the job.

3. **Be specific about your concerns.** "Yesterday you left the dishes in the sink rather than putting them in the dishwasher, and you folded the laundry but then left it on the bed rather than putting it away as I had asked. There was still an hour left in the day and Caitlin was occupied watching TV."

4. **Recognize that their previous employer may have done things differently.** "And this may have been OK in your last job, but . . ."

5. **Explain exactly what you need.** "For *our* job, we need someone really proactive. We want someone who completes a task—so if the laundry gets done, it gets folded and put away. You don't need to ask my permission, just go ahead and do it. So today, we'd like to work on this."

6. **Give the nanny a chance to share any concerns she has.** "Please also be honest and tell us about any concerns you have, so that we can address them and have the best chance of making this work."

Day Two Recap: Assessing What You've Learned

After you've completed day two, ask yourself the following questions:

• Did she pass the tests you set for her based on your concerns from the first day?
• What did she do well?
• What did she not do well?
• Do you have any new concerns?
• Do you feel that you could effectively work together?
• With all of the information that you have, could you hire this nanny tomorrow?

If you still have concerns at the end of day two, you can either do another trial with the nanny to see if she further improves, or weigh the pros and cons against your list of Musts and decide if the cons are something you can live with. If you were concerned about proactivity on day one, and she *still* was not proactive—even after your guidance—on day two, don't expect that this can be corrected going forward. Instead, you will need to decide if this particular con is make-or-break given her pros and what you feel is most important.

The Big Decision: To Hire or Not to Hire?

Sometimes the results of a trial will be very clear, and you will come away from it with a definite "Yes, we love her," or a definite "No, she's not for us." But what about the trials that have a mixed result? If there are some really wonderful things about the nanny, but she has one or two flaws that prevent her from being your absolute ideal, how do you decide whether or not to move forward?

In these cases, I always tell my clients to refer back to their ultimate goal of Constancy of Care. Remember, *Constancy of Care* means having a stable, loving, and responsive caregiver who can meet all of your child's physical, emotional, and developmental needs when you are not present. So while every nanny will have pros and cons, the Gold Standard rule is that the nanny's pros plus her cons *must still equal* Constancy of Care. If one of the nanny's cons—for example, a very quiet, timid personality—will leave your child feeling a void while you are gone, and therefore his developmental needs aren't being met, then he will not be getting Constancy of Care. But if you are at home with your child, and you can compensate for the nanny's reserve by engaging and playing with your child while she focuses more on household tasks, there may be no void at all. In general, the

more time you are going to be away from your child, the more important it is that the nanny be able to provide Constancy of Care and
meet all of your child's needs completely on her own.

Recognize also that there may be some scenarios where it is in
your child's best interest to let your own needs go. If you find a wonderful nanny who will shower your child with love and affection, and
engage him in all the right ways, you may decide that you don't mind
that she cannot cook or keep the house tidy. Make sure, however, that
you feel truly at peace with the compromise because if you are getting
shortchanged on your end, it can set the stage for problems. If the
nanny is amazing with your child but disorganized or chronically late
for work, the resulting stress and tension can affect the entire household. Before you decide to compromise, play out the scenario in your
head and ask yourself, "If I compromise on this, what is the ripple
effect? Will it impact my child for better or worse?"

BACKGROUND CHECKS: THE FINAL TEST

Even if a nanny blows you away during a trial and you are completely convinced that you have found The One, you should
always do a thorough background check before you proceed
to make an offer. No matter how great a candidate looks on
paper, she is still a virtual stranger who will be coming into
your home to care for your child. There are a number of reliable national companies that specialize in detailed background
checks for nannies, such as the Childcare Background Research Corporation (childcarebackground.com), and the cost
is generally reasonable ($100 to $200). It can be tempting to
skip this step, especially if you're pressed for time, but I truly
believe that you can *never* be too careful when it comes to the
safety of your child.

At the end of the day, trust your gut, and choose the person who appears to meet the greatest number of needs or Musts from your FNA. If something doesn't feel right about the match, *don't* force it, even if you are pressed for time and needed to hire someone yesterday. Give yourself time for another trial or even time to source some additional candidates. Trust me when I tell you that there are always more nannies out there, so keep looking until you find the right one.

Making the Offer

When you've found a nanny who you're excited about, the final step is to make her an offer. In my experience, the single best way to lay the groundwork for a healthy and happy working relationship is to structure your offer as a Nanny–Family Work Agreement. A Work Agreement is a document similar to an offer letter that spells out all the details of the job: the salary and benefits, the hours, the duties, your rules and Deal-Breakers, as well as any requests from the nanny. This is not a legally binding contract, and it can be changed or ended at any time, but it sets clear guidelines and expectations from the get-go so that everyone is on the same page.

The good news is that because you've already done such a thorough job of outlining your Musts and Deal-Breakers throughout the process, there should be very few surprises for the nanny when you finally decide to offer her the position. The only major piece that's left to discuss and agree upon is salary. If you already know from Basic Screening and the Interview that you and the nanny are on the same page in terms of salary, then you are ready to move forward. But if the nanny initially asked for more money than you can afford, you will need to have one more conversation with her to see whether her initial "magic number" has changed. You should ask, "Based on everything you now know about our family and what we are looking for, what would you need in terms of salary to do the job?" If her number has changed, or if she indicates that she is willing to bend depending on what you offer, that's good news. But if it hasn't, then you will need to decide if she is worth the financial stretch given everything you know about her skills and experience, and her performance during the trial.

Be warned, however, that I have seen situations where the family stretched beyond their means to hire a nanny they really wanted and ended up resenting the nanny for it. No matter how wonderful the nanny was, every time they wrote that check with the extra $100, they felt bitter. You don't want to put yourself or the nanny in that situation, so if you truly have a fixed or limited budget, I strongly recommend that you stick to it. Fortunately, if you've followed my process and trialed multiple candidates, you should have at least one viable backup waiting in the wings if you can't reach an agreement with your first choice.

CREATING A NANNY–FAMILY WORK AGREEMENT

Before you officially make the offer, you want to draft your Nanny–Family Work Agreement. A Work Agreement should include all of the physical logistics of your job, as well as a detailed job description that lists all of the nanny's major duties and responsibilities. You can download a Work Agreement template from my website, tammygold .com, or write up your own agreement if that's easier.

Any Work Agreement should include the following:

- Your name and contact information
- The nanny's name and contact information
- Nanny's start date and official employment anniversary (to be used when paying bonuses and giving raises)

- Days and hours for the position (These are what will be considered the standard hours, covered by the nanny's weekly base salary.)
- Summer days and hours (if different from the rest of the year)
- Weekly salary
- Overtime rate (as well as an explanation of what counts as overtime); weekend, travel, or summer pay rates if applicable
- Annual bonus
- Any additional compensation or perks
- Benefits
- Vacation days and vacation policy (Can the nanny choose her vacation weeks, or does one week have to overlap with your vacation? How much advance notice do you need?)
- Paid holidays
- Personal days and personal day policy (How do you want the nanny to handle asking for a day off? How much advance notice do you need?)
- Sick days and sick day policy (How do you want the nanny to handle a day that she is sick? When does she need to let you know— the night before? By 6 a.m.?)
- Job description (A nanny is much more likely to do what you ask if you make her responsibilities official and put them in writing. The job description should clearly list all the duties required of the nanny, whether they are for you, your children, your family, or your home.)
- Commute/transportation policy (Any details about reimbursement for gas or other transportation costs, as well as a late-night travel policy.)
- House rules (Any major house rules, such as limits on TV or the use of a cell phone; or, for a live-in situation, if the nanny needs to be in her room after a certain time at night.)
- Confidentiality (It is a good idea to include a blanket statement

about confidentiality, such as "You agree that you will not discuss our family and the details of our household or personal life with anyone, including your friends, family, or other nannies.")

- Grounds for immediate termination (Anything that you consider to be a fireable offense; you can refer back to your FNA and list of Deal-Breakers for ideas about what to include.)
- Requests by nanny (It is very important to give the nanny a chance to add her requests and conditions as well. For example, nannies often ask that the parents call at least one hour in advance if they are going to be late coming home. They may also ask for things like a weekly meeting to discuss the children, a lock on their bedroom door if they are going to be live-in, reimbursement for any snacks they may buy for the children, etc.)
- A place for both of you to sign and date

NEGOTIATING: THE ART OF GIVE-AND-TAKE

If you present your offer and the nanny agrees right away, or if she has only a few minor requests that are easy to accommodate, then you're all set and ready to sign the Work Agreement. But what if she doesn't accept your initial offer, and comes back to you asking for more substantial changes? What if she now says that she wants a higher salary, or makes a request that you can't agree to?

If you have to negotiate, the best and most effective strategy is to be as open and honest as possible about your situation and any constraints that you have: "We think you're terrific and we wish we could pay you this rate, but with our salaries and student loans, if we pay you that much, we will be running a deficit each week." Sharing your story and letting them know why you can't meet her number or give her extra vacation will go a long way. I've been negotiating with nannies on behalf of parents for many years, and in my experience, nannies will almost always be accommodating once they understand where the parents are coming from. You can also try to come up with a few additional perks that will add value to your compensation package. If you make it clear that you understand the nanny's worth and are trying to make up the difference elsewhere, it is possible that she will come around.

However, if you are not being honest about your circumstances, and are just holding to a lower salary on principle, or because you are trying to get a "good deal," nannies will spot it a mile off. They will look at the house you live in, the cars you drive, the shoes you wear, the kinds of things you buy for your children, and they will know that you are being dishonest. I had one nanny tell me, "The family totally lied to me. They told me they couldn't afford to pay me what I made at my last job, but after I started working there, I saw them redecorate their house and redo the kitchen with top-of-the-line everything. It made me so mad and I wanted to say to them, 'I'm caring for your daughter, I'm taking her to school, I'm tutoring her, I'm loving her, I'm holding her when she's sick, and you can't pay me the extra $50 a week—but you can redo your entire kitchen?'" That kind of discrepancy breeds resentment and will set you up for trouble down the line.

When negotiating about salary, you should also beware of the nanny who agrees to a lower number, but then jacks up the rates for nights, weekends, and overtime because she knows that you have unpredictable hours and sees that as a way to get more money. Unless you have a very reliable schedule, don't agree to higher overtime rates just to get your nanny to agree to a lower base. You may very well end up paying her far more money than if you'd just given her the extra $75 a week.

The key to a successful negotiation is to work toward both sides being happy. This means that you may have to give a little on your end, and the nanny may have to give a little as well. My general rule of thumb is: If you can honor the nanny's request without compromising on your child's needs or your parental needs in a significant way, and without putting undue pressure on yourself, then do it—because when a nanny feels happy and appreciated, she will pay it back to the family tenfold. You can also use her request as leverage to negotiate for something that is beneficial for you. For example, if she wants to occasionally bring her own child to work on Fridays, and you agree, as long as she is willing to give you $50 off of her weekly

---

WHEN IT'S WORTH IT TO PAY MORE

I truly believe that when it comes to good childcare, you can never pay too much, as long as you can afford it. A truly great nanny translates into you being a better parent, you and your partner having a better relationship, and your child being happier and receiving everything he needs developmentally to reach his full potential.

But—and this is a big "but"—paying extra is only worth it if the quality of care and the nanny's commitment to your family warrants it. Put simply, it is worth going a little bit above for a nanny who is willing to go a little bit above for you. I have seen plenty of nannies who want maximum pay but will only do the bare minimum for you and your child. These are the nannies who say, "I want this number, but I'm not doing your laundry, and I'm only cooking for the kids, and I'm only tidying up the playroom." The nanny worth stretching for is the nanny who will stay late once in a while and not charge you overtime, and who will pitch in and do whatever is needed to help the family, regardless of whether the task was in her original job description. If a nanny isn't going to push herself for you, there is no reason to push yourself for her.

---

salary whenever it happens, then the arrangement can benefit you both.

Before you agree to any changes, do your best to project and think as far ahead as possible. Maybe you can agree to give her more vacation this year, but will you be in the same position a year from now if you change jobs or go back to work full-time? If you're not certain, make it clear in your Work Agreement that this particular arrangement will need to be revisited on an annual basis. Be sure to add any brand-new deal points to your Work Agreement as well, so you and the nanny both have a written record of what has been amended and agreed to.

Congratulations, you did it! You found and hired your perfect nanny, and now you can finally put the search behind you. In the last part of the book, we'll look at how to set your nanny up for success, and how to ensure smooth sailing in the months and years to come.

PART THREE

Working Together As Your Children Grow

CHAPTER 8

———•———

The Magic of Training

How to Create a Gold Standard Nanny

I always tell my clients that the single biggest factor in whether or not a nanny succeeds is the amount of involvement and training that the parents give her when she starts. As I've said before, it doesn't matter if she has been a nanny for a hundred years, she has never been a nanny in *your* home before. If you don't take the time to show her your way and give her tools, she will do things her own way, or the way she did them for her previous family. And if you don't train your nanny and she doesn't deliver or makes mistakes, then she is not responsible—*you* are.

If you followed my Gold Standard hiring process, you have already provided your nanny with some basic training during the trials. Now that she is officially working for you, it's time to take it to the next level. Don't ever assume that your nanny has learned everything she needs to know during the hiring process because it is impossible to go over every single detail or contingency in such a short period of time. On-the-job training is what shapes and sharpens your nanny's

Secrets of the Nanny Whisperer

raw skills and abilities, and transforms her into the caregiver who is able to meet all of your needs and your child's needs in an ideal way. If you are coming to this chapter and you already have a nanny and you are looking for ways to improve the situation, training—or *re*-training the Gold Standard way, using the tools in this chapter—can make a huge amount of difference in a nanny's performance. Very often, training alone can raise a caregiver from being a so-so, B-level nanny to an A.

The key to successfully training your nanny is to arm her with as much information as possible by creating what I call a Family Handbook. Based on a series of forms that I give to clients, the Family Handbook is designed to compile *all* of the essential details about

---

IF YOU ALREADY HAVE A NANNY

Retraining your current nanny can be a very effective way to improve her overall performance. You can use an anniversary (such as six months or a year) to introduce the Family Handbook and say, "I recently read a book that made me realize that I did not give you the best training when you started. I'm so sorry about this, and I'd like to do so now so that we can work together even more effectively. I've created this handbook so that you always have good, clear directions, and I'd like us to go over everything again and get your thoughts so that we can both be happy with this situation for a long time."

If you are retraining, the sections that spell out rules and the daily schedule in the Family Handbook will be the most important. The daily schedule in particular allows you to correct and define your nanny's routine and tell her exactly what you want her to be doing and when. You should also do all the steps in basic training, including setting up a Communication Log.

---

your family in one place, and to serve as a guidebook that the nanny can refer back to while she is on the job. Putting your instructions in writing is the very best way to set or reset expectations, keep things professional, and ensure that there is no cause for confusion when you're not there. When a nanny has clear guidelines and instructions for every single aspect of the job, she is far less likely to slack off, be forgetful, or stray from your wishes because the expectations are right in front of her—no excuses.

Creating Your Family Handbook

Nannies often say to me, "Tammy, I will do whatever the parents want, but I wish they would just *tell me* what that is—clearly and honestly—so I don't feel uncomfortable."

If you were starting a new job, you would expect to receive some sort of training or orientation, and nannies—even very experienced nannies—are no different. You need to tell your nanny how you want her to do the job, and the more training you give her, the better she will be. Your Family Handbook should provide detailed instructions about what the nanny and your child can and cannot do and how you want her to handle every single aspect of the day. Otherwise, how is she going to know that your child is not allowed to use the iPad in the car or that she is not allowed to buy him ice cream at the park? Even if you feel like you've already given your nanny a lot of direction, trust me when I say that giving instruction on the fly is very different from presenting it in written form. There is something about putting your directions and rules in writing that elevates their level of importance. The nanny will understand that you take them very seriously and you eliminate the possibility she will improvise or make mistakes simply because she's afraid to ask you how you want something done.

If you are hiring a parental unit nanny, thorough training is mandatory before you start working. Otherwise, the nanny will be unprepared, and she will have no one to turn to for guidance throughout the day. If you are hiring a partner or an executor nanny, you can usually take a little bit more time with training because you will be at home to answer questions. However, you should still complete the Family Handbook because it is important to provide any nanny with as much concrete information as possible.

Here is what should be included in your Family Handbook:

PARENT AND EMERGENCY CONTACT INFORMATION

For each parent, you want to include the following:

- Name
- Cell phone number and email
- Employer's name and address
- Work phone and extension
- Name of assistant and assistant's phone number, if appropriate

You should also provide names and contact information for neighbors, friends, or family in the area that the nanny could reach

---

SHORTCUT: DOWNLOAD THE GOLD STANDARD FAMILY HANDBOOK

Creating your own customized version of the Family Handbook is best, because every family is unique. However, if you don't want to spend time typing up questions and making charts, you can download a complete, easy-to-fill-in version from my website, tammygold.com.

out to for help if you are unavailable. If both you and your partner work and do not spend a great deal of time at your desks, you should refer the nanny to an assistant or coworker whom they can call in an emergency.

HOUSEHOLD INFORMATION

If you are hiring a parental unit nanny, or have a partner or executor nanny who will be left alone in your home for longer periods of time, you should give her as much information as possible about your home and how it operates. Emergencies happen, and your nanny needs to know who to call if the alarm goes off or a pipe bursts. You should provide information on the following:

- **Security:** If you have a security system, she will need the keypad number, alarm password, and the security company name and phone number. Other related items may include garage door password, location of extra keys, or phone number of the front desk or doorman.
- **Utilities:** Contact information for your cable TV provider, phone provider, Internet provider, electricity provider, gas/oil provider,

CREATE A 911 PROTOCOL

People don't always think clearly in an emergency, and many nannies are trying to function in a second language, so you can help your nanny by creating a script for calling 911 that includes your address, phone number, cross streets, and another clear point of location to give to responders. Rather than including it in your handbook, I recommend posting it on the refrigerator and near all telephones.

water provider, and trash/recycling service. Other related items may include fuse box location, water cutoff valve location, thermostat locations, and any directions about household temperature settings.

- **Household services:** Names and contact information for housekeeper, handyman, electrician, plumber, heating and air-conditioning repair, appliance repair, lawn care, pool care, and pest control.
- **Animal care:** Any information related to the care of your pet, such as veterinarian, pet store, local animal hospital, groomer, and location of a dog run.
- **Care and retail:** Names and addresses of any shops or businesses where your nanny may need to run errands during the day, such as dry cleaners, grocery store, deli, bakery, drugstore/pharmacy, florist, post office, pet store, hardware store, and clothing stores.

HOUSE RULES

House rules are the general rules of your home that do not relate directly to the care of your child, such as:

- Any rooms in your home that are off limits or that have doors to be kept closed.
- Visitor policy: If the nanny is having a personal visitor, does she need your approval?
- Door policy: Do you want the nanny to open the door to strangers when you are not there?
- Rules about coming and going, such as always locking the door behind you, always closing the garage door, putting keys in a certain place, or removing shoes as soon as you come into the house.
- Specific rules for a live-in, such as what time she should go to her room for the evening, when she can use the kitchen, whether or not

she can eat with the family, and whether she has a curfew. How will she know when it's family time vs. time when you need her?

TRAVEL AND TRANSPORTATION RULES

You need to specify the general rules about how, when, and where the nanny may travel with your children outside your home as well as any rules that apply while they are out. Your transportation rules might include the following:

- **By car:** Which car the nanny should use, your car seat/seatbelt policy, who pays for gas, and when and where the nanny is allowed to drive your child. Does she need to be home by a certain time? You may also want to provide some general rules, such as:
  - Never talk on a cell phone while you are driving.
  - Never leave the children in the car without supervision.
  - "If you are dropping the older child off and the baby is sleeping, wake the baby and bring her with you as you walk the older child to the door."

- **By bus/subway:** Which lines and routes the nanny may use, and at what times—for example, how far away can the nanny travel with your child? Are there times of day that you would prefer that she not use public transportation, such as rush hour? Who pays for the fares?

- **By taxi:** When your nanny is allowed to travel by cab with your children and how far away they may go, who pays the fare, and safety rules such as wearing seatbelts and whether or not to bring a car seat.

- **By foot/stroller:** When and where the nanny is allowed to walk with your child, how far from your home they are allowed to go, and if there are certain streets or areas that are off limits. You may also include safety rules: "When you cross the street, please have Ben walk his scooter across rather than riding it."

• **General rules for leaving the house:** This section would include rules such as the following:

   - What the nanny should bring with her whenever she leaves the house with your child, for example diaper bag, sippy cups, snacks, sunscreen, hand sanitizer, $20 from the petty cash jar.
   - "If you need to take the children on an emergency personal errand, you must notify me first."
   - "Text me to let me know where the children are when you are not at home."

YOUR CHILD 101

A major factor in achieving Constancy of Care and creating a situation in which your nanny can be her best is to tell her *everything* about your child, and be as detailed and thorough as possible. For each child, you want to create an in-depth profile that includes the following:

Basic Information

• Your child's full name, and any nickname
• Age and date of birth
• Social Security number
• Height and weight (weight is very important for proper dosing of medications and should be updated every six to twelve months, depending on age)
• Blood type
• Allergies
• Chronic medical conditions or recent surgeries

Medical Information

- Name of pediatrician and contact information, including phone number and address
- Health insurance information (you should make a copy of your insurance card to give your nanny to keep in several places, such as her wallet and the diaper bag)
- Preferred hospital and address for emergencies
- Name of dentist and contact information
- Medical authorization-to-treat form, which allows your nanny to give permission to doctors or a hospital to treat your children in your absence
- Medications, including any medications that your child takes on a daily basis as well as those that may be administered as needed (acetaminophen, ibuprofen, allergy medications, saline sprays)

If English is the nanny's second language, being extra clear about medications is essential—for example, the nanny may not know that Tylenol is the same as acetaminophen and that it is used for fevers or headaches. Even writing the uses directly on the package or bottle with an indelible marker can be a good idea.

For every medication, you should list the name (generic and brand), the dose, when to administer, and any special instructions in your Family Handbook:

Medication: Children's ibuprofen (also called Children's Motrin)

Dosage: 2 teaspoons

When to administer: Every six hours as needed for fevers, headaches, colds, or sore throats

Special instructions: Tommy needs to take the ibuprofen with milk or it upsets his stomach. Please note the time that you administer it on the calendar.

If your nanny will be giving medications on a regular basis, I suggest creating and using a daily Medicine Log. This form can be found on my website, tammygold.com.

School Information

- Name of school, along with address, phone number, and website
- Grade/class
- Name of your child's teacher(s) and contact information
- Name of school nurse and contact information
- School hours (make sure to note any day-to-day variations for after-school clubs and so on)
- Instructions for dropoff and pickup
- Any carpool information, along with names of other kids and contact information for each parent
- Information about meals at school—for example, does the nanny need to pack a lunch or a snack, and on what days?

Activity Information

For each of your child's activities, you want to list the following:

- Name of activity (for example, soccer)
- Days and times (both start time and end time)
- Start date and end date
- Location and contact information
- Instructor
- Attire
- Additional items to bring (such as a water bottle and sports equipment)

- Any carpool information, along with names of other kids and contact information for each parent

Approved Free Activities and Play Areas

You should list places where your nanny can take your children during any free time, including parks, playgrounds, kids' gyms, and your local YMCA. For each place, be sure to include the following:

- Name and address
- Hours of operation and your preferred time to go
- Information about what to wear or bring (for example, socks for the kids' gym)
- Any rules for these locations, such as "Please keep Jenna on the toddler playground for now. She will try to run over to the big kids' one, but she can't safely manage the bigger jungle gym just yet."

Approved Playdates

It is helpful to provide your nanny with a list of approved playdates whom she can contact when the children are bored and ready for company. For each friend, you want to include the following:

- Child's name
- Parent's/caregiver's names and contact information
- Child's home address
- Any additional information about scheduling or the other child, such as "Todd can play only on Tuesdays and Fridays," or "Todd is allergic to eggs."

You may also want to include any general rules you have regarding playdates, such as:

- "Please notify me twenty-four hours in advance when a child is coming over for a playdate."
- "When leaving Tommy for a playdate, please confirm that another adult will be home."
- "No playdates with sick children."

Personality Profile

The profile section is designed to provide your nanny with an overview of your child's personality as well as practical suggestions and helpful hints for understanding him and interacting with him in a positive way. To create the profile, answer the following questions:

- What activities does your child like to do?
- What toys does your child like to play with?
- How can the nanny best engage this child? How can the nanny encourage interaction?
- Are there certain things that the nanny should *not* do or say to this child?
- What is the child's naptime/bedtime ritual? What steps should the nanny follow for putting this child to bed?
- Does your child have any chores or daily responsibilities?
- What is the best way to resolve conflict for this child? Through *positive* encouragements or rewards (such as an extra book at bedtime, an extra cookie, thirty minutes of videogames) or by *negative* reinforcements or punishments (serve dessert only if he eats three bites of vegetables; if he throws toys, take them away)?
- Under what circumstances should the nanny use a time-out (for example, when the child hits others)?
- Under what circumstances may the nanny call you?

CHILDCARE RULES

Write out the rules specifically relating to your children and their care that you would like your nanny to follow when you are gone. You may include rules about the following:

- **Bath time,** such as "Both children should have a bath each day and a shampoo twice a week," "Jenna has dry skin, so use the Cetaphil lotion daily," or "Please wipe down the bathroom countertop afterward."
- **TV and screen time,** such as "No TV or computer until *after* homework is done, and then for only one hour."
- **Activity guidelines,** such as "Please read at least three books a day" or "Sarah enjoys her play mat in small doses, but after fifteen minutes she gets overstimulated."
- **Cleaning up,** such as "Tommy should pick up his room every night before bed" or "Please vacuum under the kitchen table at the end of the day before you leave."
- **Nonacceptable behavior:** Behaviors that are not allowed under any circumstances, such as hitting, biting, throwing the ball in the house, or speaking disrespectfully.
- **Communicating with parents,** such as "Keep the baby log updated throughout the day" or "Call Mom immediately if one of the children is not feeling well."

FOOD AND MEALTIMES

Rules and wishes regarding food are a major issue for many parents. If you have very specific ideas about what and how your child should eat, you need to take the time to communicate your preferences to the nanny and provide her with as much practical information as possible. Some parents will go as far as creating weekly menus for the nanny to follow. At minimum, you should give her guidance on the following:

- Allergies or special dietary needs
- Food likes and dislikes
- Food rules, such as "No sweets after 4 p.m."
- Protocol for introducing new foods, if applicable
- Meal preparation rules, such as "Every meal must have at least one fruit and one veggie" or "Please slice all grapes and cherry tomatoes in half to prevent choking."
- Mealtime rules, such as "Children must wash their hands before eating" or "Children must eat at least half of what is on their plate."
- Mealtime rules for the *nanny*, such as "Nanny can prepare her meal as soon as the children are all eating at the table" or "Nanny must prepare her meal at the same time so that they can all eat at the table together."
- Provide several options for each meal (including snacks and desserts) for each child, such as "For dinner please serve chicken and veggies, pasta and meatballs, or salmon and potatoes."
- Desired meal schedule and times

DAILY SCHEDULE

So many times, parents have asked me, "What should my nanny do all day?" The answer is that you need to tell her what to do, and it is very helpful if you put together a daily schedule for the nanny to follow, especially if you have multiple children who will have different needs at different times. Your schedule can be as specific as you want, right down to the types of activities you would like your child to be doing and when, such as crafts, or sitting in the bouncy seat, or playing outside. This kind of schedule can also be extremely helpful if you aren't happy with how your nanny has been stimulating your child or structuring the day. I recommend breaking up the day by hours (you may want to do every half hour for infants, who have a short attention span), and listing the nanny's to-dos by child, as shown in the chart that follows.

Daily Household Tasks for Nanny

In addition to outlining what you would like the nanny to do for your child, you should also provide her with a list of the household tasks that she is responsible for each day, such as:

- Feed and give the dog fresh water in the morning and at night.
- Clean up the kitchen after meals and load the dishes into the dishwasher.
- Add any items we are low on to the grocery list on the refrigerator.
- Restock the diaper changing station at the end of the day.

WEEKLY SCHEDULE

In addition to a daily schedule, I recommend creating a weekly calendar or schedule that everyone in the family, including the nanny, can refer to. Your weekly schedule should focus on the big picture events, such as activities, playdates, birthday parties, doctor's appointments, and anything else that doesn't happen every day. Your weekly schedule should look something like the chart that follows.

Weekly Tasks for Nanny

In addition to creating a weekly schedule that everyone in the family can be aware of and follow, you should also provide the nanny with a list of any *weekly*—rather than daily—tasks that she is responsible

DAILY SCHEDULE			
	TOMMY (7 Years)	JENNA (4 Years)	SARAH (9 Months)	PARENTS
6 a.m.			6:30: wake up, change diaper, bottle, dress	
7 a.m.	7:15: wake up, get dressed, brush teeth, make bed	7:30: wake up, get dressed, brush teeth 7:45: take medicine	7:10: put in swing or Pack'N Play with toys while you help Jenna and Tommy	7:00: Dad leaves 7:30: Mom leaves
8 a.m.	8:00: breakfast 8:30: school bus picks up	8:00: breakfast 8:45: drop off at school	8:00: put in bouncy seat next to kitchen table while Jenna and Tommy eat breakfast	
9 a.m.			9:00: breakfast 9:30: naptime	

for. These might include putting the trash and recycling out on Monday night before she leaves or preparing a meal plan for the following week so the parents can pick up groceries over the weekend.

WEEKLY SCHEDULE

MONDAY 24	TUESDAY 25	WEDNESDAY 26
11:30 a.m. Sarah: Little Rockers 3:15 p.m. Jenna: gymnastics	9–12 p.m. housekeeper 4:00 p.m. Tommy: no karate this week! 4:30 p.m. Jenna: Dr. Wallace checkup	1:20 p.m. Sarah: Little Ones Tumbling 4:00 p.m. Tommy: playdate with Todd Redmond (his mom will drop him off)

THURSDAY 27	FRIDAY 28	SATURDAY 29	SUNDAY 30
9–12 p.m. housekeeper 4:30 p.m. Jenna: ballet 7:00 p.m. Mom and Dad: date night	Mom working from home 1:00 p.m. Lawn company 4:00 p.m. Sarah: story hour at library 5:30 p.m. Parent–nanny weekly check-in	1 p.m. Sarah: Maggie Stanford's birthday party at Skatium roller rink	2 p.m. Tommy: tennis

Basic Training

If you've already done two days of trials, your home and daily routine should be somewhat familiar to your nanny. Even so, you never want to just throw her into the mix, so here are the essentials that you should cover. If you are retraining an existing nanny, you should do *everything* described below, with the exception of the tour. Don't assume that she knows it all already—you will do better to start fresh at square one and teach her exactly how you want things done.

- **Give her another quick tour of your home.** Show her how to open and operate any doors, safety gates, alarm systems, and appliances (such as the coffeemaker or dishwasher) that may require an explanation.
- **Review the Family Handbook together.** After the tour, you should sit down and go over everything together, including the daily

---

STARTING OFF RIGHT: WELCOMING A NEW NANNY

On the day that your nanny starts work, be sure to welcome her warmly into your home. For live-ins, a neatly made bed with comfy pillows, and maybe a mini-fridge or basket stocked with snacks and drinks, will help her feel at ease. I always tell parents that in addition to a bed and a dresser, a television is mandatory for live-in nannies because everyone likes to relax and zone out, especially if they are stuck in a room for twelve hours. Other items that will be greatly appreciated are a computer, so she can check email or Skype with family at home, and books and magazines. If the nanny is live-out, you might buy the coffee she likes or leave her some snacks or special foods for lunch.

Beyond making her feel welcome, the most important thing you can give to your nanny during those first few days is time. You should spend as much time with her as possible so that she will be getting into a groove by the time you need to leave. Spending a good amount of time together is also crucial because it allows you to get a sense of the nanny's personality and demeanor. The more you can observe her and get a sense of her typical tone and behavior, the better equipped you will be to notice any changes and address any unhappiness, stress, or other issues before they become a problem.

---

and weekly schedules, so that she has an opportunity to ask questions.

- **If she will be driving, teach her how to operate the car.** It is essential that you make sure that the nanny is comfortable driving your vehicle and that she understands how to use the safety belts and car seats, as well as the GPS system, if you have one. You may also want to take her on a dry run to any places that she will be driving to frequently, such as school, the park, or the grocery store.

- **Train, train, train.** Just like you did in the trials, walk the nanny through every piece of your daily routine and give her as much direction as possible about how you want things done. Remember that details are one of the keys to achieving Constancy of Care: By teaching your nanny to do things just like you, right down to songs you sing to the baby before she takes her nap, you will make sure that your child retains a sense of consistency and stability and never feels a drop in the level of care or affection when you're not there. This kind of training can be done *at any time* and can help to improve a lackluster nanny situation.

- **Decide when the nanny will eat.** It may sound silly, but when a nanny is working long hours and caring for multiple children, she literally may not have a moment in the day to eat. There are also many nannies who won't eat unless the parents actually tell them to, so take some time now to look over the daily schedule and figure out together when she can realistically eat meals.

- **Decide how you will handle the end of the day.** I have heard parents complain a million times, "Tammy, she just sits there when my husband comes home from work, when it's clear that this is our family time and she should leave." But I've also heard equally as many times, "Tammy, as soon as I walk in the door, she's gone. It's like the minute I arrive home, she's off duty." Parents grumble all the time that their nanny stays too late or leaves too quickly, but your nanny will have no idea what you want her to do unless you tell her. Mornings are easier, because everyone knows exactly what time the job starts, but you need to figure out what kind of overlap—if any—you want at the end of the day. This is especially important for live-in situations, where the nanny may not have anyplace else to go. You will need to talk to your nanny about the following issues:

- Do you want her to stay to help with the kids even after both parents are home?
- Do you want to hear about the day right then, or would you rather she communicate her updates at a different time or in a different way (for example, by using a daily Communication Log)?

• **Create a daily Communication Log.** If you are one of those parents who prefers to do the handoff and doesn't have the energy for an in-depth conversation about the kids when you get home, a daily Communication Log can be a terrific, easy way to exchange information with your nanny about your child's day. You should complete the parent part with any special notes or instructions for the nanny the night before, and then the nanny can respond to your notes and leave any additional ones in the nanny part throughout the day. You can download a blank log from my website, tammygold.com.

Transitioning the Nanny with Your Children

Bonding with children takes time, so don't be concerned if your nanny doesn't form an amazing connection with your child overnight. A good nanny will take her lead from the child: If the child is instantly affectionate and wants to give her a hug, the nanny should embrace him with open arms. If the child is hesitant, the nanny should respect that and give him space to warm up slowly. Here are some strategies that you can use to help your nanny connect with children of different ages:

- **For an infant:** Spend as much time with your nanny and baby as possible, so that your baby sees Mom and this new person together. Do your entire daily routine with the nanny at your side, and then on day two, share the responsibilities with your nanny— for example, you start the feeding and then let the nanny finish it. On day three, have the nanny do the entire routine while you watch in the same room. After that, you can leave for short periods of time, but make sure that you always reappear fairly soon in the beginning so that your baby sees and understands that you always come back.

- **For a toddler:** You and your nanny should approach your child together and then have the nanny propose a fun activity: "Alex, can you show me your trucks?" or "Can I play blocks with you, Leo?" Toddlers need to see the nanny as a playmate first, so the more time you can set aside to have your nanny focus on playing with your child while you are present, the better. Also, toddlers love treats, so if the nanny can give your child a cookie or do a fun activity with him like making ice-cream sundaes, it will be a surefire way to win the child over.

- **For a preschooler:** Give your nanny an activity or tell her about something that your child loves and have her approach your child with it. For example, you might tell the nanny to say, "Clara, I heard that you love the movie *Frozen*, and I do too. Would you like to do this *Frozen* puzzle with me?" You could also purchase a brand-new toy ahead of time, and let the nanny be the one to present and introduce it, and help your child play with it for the very first time.

- **For an older child or tween:** Having the nanny and child go to a fun event together can be a great way to help them bond. You should have the nanny invite your child so that your child sees it as her idea. For example, you can have the nanny say, "Mindy, your mom said that you are dying to see the new Justin Bieber movie. Would you like to go this afternoon?"
- **For a teenager:** Teens can be tough for a new nanny to win over but doing activities together like shopping or going to the movies or a local sports game may help your teen and the nanny bond. Making sure that the nanny hears and respects him, and treats him like a young adult rather than a child, will help him come around.

Above all, make sure that you always listen to the feedback that your children give you about the nanny, especially when the feedback comes from younger children. If there is something that your child says that he doesn't like about the nanny, share it with the nanny (as long as it's rational) so that you can work together to help her build a connection with your child.

Going Forward

Beyond the first day, there will be many opportunities to fine-tune your child's care as well as your working relationship with your nanny. The most important things are to keep the lines of communication open and recognize that the arrangement is a work in progress. Here are some ways to keep things running smoothly or to facilitate a better working relationship with your current nanny:

• **Establish a Weekly Check-In:** It is very important to check in with your nanny often to make sure that everything is going OK. If you are at home or are at home part-time, you may find that it is easy to communicate with your nanny about how she is feeling and to share feedback and ideas regarding your child. But if you are gone sixty hours a week, it is essential that you make time to catch up with your nanny face to face. A regular check-in gives you the opportunity to present any positive feedback or criticisms you may have—for example, "We love how wonderful you are with our daughter, but on

---

TEACHING YOUR CHILDREN TO RESPECT THE NANNY

Some parents are worried that having a nanny will spoil their children and that always having another person picking up after them will teach their children to expect or demand it. But having a nanny will not make your children spoiled unless you let it. Here are some preventative measures:

1. **Demand from an early age that your child respect the nanny always.** As with all adults, *yes* is always followed by *please*, and *no* is always followed by *thank you*. The lesson is that people from all backgrounds and ethnicities deserve respect, as do people with all types of jobs.

2. **As your child grows, have him do more to help the nanny.** Tell the nanny, "You may place the laundry in Sarah's room so she can put it away" or "Now that Ryan is six, he will clear and scrape his own plate."

3. **Help him take time to appreciate the nanny.** For example, create a character-building lesson on empathy by asking your child, "Since Rosemary doesn't have children of her own, how do you think we can make her feel special on Mother's Day?"

Wednesday you were a little late, which meant that I missed my train, so that's something we really need you to work on." You also want to hear from your nanny to make sure she is happy with how things are going. Some nannies may be cautious about giving honest feedback to an employer, so you may need to reassure them: "We really want to hear about how things are going for you, so please do not be afraid to speak your mind." A regular check-in also ensures that problems don't have a chance to fester. If she does something that bugs you, you know that you will have the opportunity to bring it up and discuss it in the proper forum.

Checking in with your nanny often is also important because your child's needs will change constantly as he grows. Parenthood is a constantly shifting ground, so what previously worked for putting your child to sleep or avoiding temper tantrums may suddenly not work anymore. As your family evolves and your child matures, you and the nanny will need to work together to make decisions about how to handle each new phase. You want to give her the chance to say, "I think he's ready for potty training. We should probably think about getting some Pull-Ups."

FRIENDS: THE NATURAL NANNY CAM

After you have finished training your nanny, it's always a good idea to have a friend stop by your apartment unannounced or have your mom drop in on the nanny unexpectedly when you're not there to see how things are going. You can also put your child and nanny in a music class or other activity with one of your friends, so that the friend can observe and report back to you. Knowing that people may come by unannounced or that you have mom friends who will be at the playground every day will keep the nanny on her toes.

• **Find Backup:** Even if you're at the end of a long search and even if you *just* finally found and hired your perfect nanny, it is never too early to think about lining up someone to take her place if she is sick or can't get to work for another unforeseen reason. If you don't have the option of staying home yourself, you will need to find someone who can step in and care for your child on very short notice, whether it's a family member, a babysitter, or a local daycare. There are also certain nanny agencies that will send a substitute nanny on short notice, but you need to be registered with them to take advantage of this service. Whatever you choose, *don't wait* to figure this out until you're in a jam. If there's one thing that can strain your relationship with your nanny and breed resentment, it's being left in the lurch with no childcare—even if no one, including your nanny, is to blame.

Even if you've done everything you can to start your nanny off on the right foot, training is only one part of a healthy nanny–parent relationship. In the next chapter, I'll teach you how to speak "nanny" so that you can continue to communicate and work together effectively to co-parent your child in the months and years ahead.

CHAPTER 9

————

How to Speak Nanny

*Communicating to Bring Out the Best
in Your Child's Caregiver*

One of the most challenging aspects of having a nanny is learning to be a boss in your own home. Even if you are used to managing people at work and feel comfortable delegating authority in the professional realm, managing an employee on the home front is very different, especially when that person is being paid to care for your child. For the relationship to work, you will need to treat your nanny with both the same professionalism and respect that you would afford a colleague and the kindness and consideration that you would afford a family member or a friend. It's a delicate dance, and for many parents one that can be difficult to master. The highly personal nature of the relationship means that emotions can run high on both sides, even over minor issues. However, if you want your nanny to succeed, you will need to learn to manage the relationship in a way that keeps your emotions in check while motivating her to respect your wishes and give her very best to your child.

The key to building a successful working relationship lies in proper communication, or what I call "nanny speak." Nanny speak refers to a way of communicating and providing feedback and direction that is easy for the nanny to understand, and leaves no room for misinterpretation or drama. In my experience, the majority of issues that arise between parents and nannies result from simple misunderstandings.

When I do nanny–family mediation, the most common complaint I hear from parents is that the nanny doesn't do things the way the mom wants them done. But the most common response that I hear from the nannies is, "I had no idea she wanted me to do that! Of course I would have done it, but she never told me." Training and using the Family Handbook will lay a great foundation, but by also learning to speak nanny, you can automatically prevent 90 percent of the problems that can crop up between you. Whether you need to correct a simple mistake that your nanny made or confront her about a larger, more serious issue, nanny speak will help you

> The majority of issues that arise between parents and nannies result from simple misunderstandings.

IS IT EVER TOO LATE TO START USING NANNY SPEAK?

Even if your nanny has been with you for several years, you can still implement the techniques in this chapter. Improving your communication can change the course of your relationship at any time and help your nanny to perform at a higher level. When you communicate well, everyone wins: You will be happier, your child will be happier, and your nanny will be happier because she feels respected and there is greater openness between you.

express your needs and wishes clearly, set a course of action, and ensure that your nanny makes changes and responds.

The Art of Speaking Clearly

Many parents feel somewhat awkward in their role as a domestic employer, and this leads them to be unclear when speaking to their nanny, particularly when correcting or giving direction. Mothers are especially prone to trepidation because of the many complex emotions that surround the nanny–mom relationship (more on this in Chapter 11). Language barriers and cultural differences as well as the blurred line between employee and friend can also contribute to miscommunication. Here are some of the common mistakes that parents make, along with my Nanny Speak Rules for parents.

RULE 1: NEVER POSE A DIRECTION AS A QUESTION

By posing your request or directive as a question—for example, "Could you throw an extra load of laundry in before you leave?"— you're giving the nanny a choice and the option of saying no. Phrases like "Could you . . ." "Would you mind . . ." or "When you have a chance, can you . . ." might sound nicer to your ears, but they leave room for misinterpretation. If something is important to you, and you really want it to get done, you need to state your needs clearly and unequivocally: "Please throw a load of laundry in before you leave."

RULE 2: NEVER USE THE WORD *IF*

A lot of moms make the mistake of qualifying their requests for the sake of being polite—for example, "If you have a minute, the recycling bins need to be put back in the garage" and "If you could

take all the 2T clothing out of Sophie's closet, that would be great."
Again, you might think it's more polite to say it this way, but the
critical word that you've introduced into your request is *if*. As with
questions, *if* leaves room for the nanny to choose whether or not
to follow through. If she's busy with other tasks, she may very
well think, "I won't worry about that; it didn't seem that important
to her."

RULE 3: IF YOU WANT THE NANNY TO DO SOMETHING, JUST TELL HER; DON'T BEAT AROUND THE BUSH

A lot of moms will talk around a topic, hoping the nanny will take
the hint—for example, "Bethany, that diaper bag looks heavy. Are
you sure you can carry it and manage Sebastian all the way to
the park? Wouldn't you rather take the stroller along too?" Moms
do this all the time. The mother sees the nanny struggling to manage
the diaper bag, the ball, the toy trucks, and her child, and she is worried that the nanny won't have enough hands to keep her child safe
while walking down the road with heavy traffic. She really wants
the nanny to take the stroller so that child can be strapped in, but
she doesn't want to seem like she's bossy or micromanaging. So instead of just telling the nanny to take the stroller, she talks around the
topic, hoping that the nanny will get the idea. But the nanny says,
"Oh no, we're fine," and then the mother worries while they are gone
and silently fumes that the nanny didn't listen. Instead of trying to
be nice, just be direct: "Sandy, I'm worried about all the traffic on
Elm Street. I would like you to take the stroller so Sebastian can be
strapped in."

One of the biggest fights that I ever had with our nanny was over a stupid incident about her shoes. We were traveling with our three kids and our nanny, Marjorie, and we were walking around the town and she was wearing these high wedge sandals. As usual, the kids were climbing all over her, and our littlest one wanted to be carried. I was nervous that Marjorie was going to fall while carrying her because I had fallen while carrying my son in similar shoes. So all day long I kept saying things like, "Marjorie, are you sure you can walk in those shoes?" "Are you sure you can run after the kids in those?" "Are you positive you feel safe? I had shoes like that once and I always felt wobbly." I just kept at it and kept at it, until finally, as we were walking to the car, she took off her shoes without a word and threw them in the trash. I felt terrible, and I realized that I'd been completely passive-aggressive, poking at the issue all day long, when I should have just said, "Marjorie, I'm concerned about you carrying Ryan in those shoes. I'll take him today, but tomorrow, I'd prefer that you wear flats."

—MELISSA, CHICAGO, IL

RULE 4: DON'T ATTRIBUTE YOUR NEEDS OR REQUEST TO SOMEONE (OR SOMETHING) ELSE

There are a lot of moms who feel uncomfortable taking ownership of their requests and directives for the nanny. They will tell the nanny things like, "Our doctor told us that it's very important not to use a cell phone near a child" or "I read an article that said you should settle a baby this way." While you may think that you are adding credibility to your request, it can actually have the opposite effect: The nanny may think, "Well, I've been a nanny for twenty years and I disagree with that article, and she didn't actually say that I needed to do it this way," and then decide to disregard the information. If you're tempted to attribute something that you want to your doctor, your friend, your mother, or even your husband, know that your request has less impact and is far less likely to be taken seriously when it's one step removed from you—the boss. Saying that something is important to someone else is not the same as saying, "This is really important to me, and here is what I need you to do."

RULE 5: DON'T GIVE FEEDBACK OR DIRECTION IN EMAILS OR TEXTS

Unless you have a young, college-educated American nanny who is used to receiving direction via email and is fluent in English and therefore fully equipped to read and process your thoughts, you should avoid delivering feedback or criticism via email or your phone. While email is the standard mode of communication in the professional world, and texting has become de rigueur as well, most nannies are uncomfortable using these methods for anything more than basic communications such as, "Please don't forget the dry cleaning," so complaining to your nanny in long, discursive messages will almost certainly be misunderstood or ignored. Furthermore, subtleties like tone and body language are completely lost when using text or email, so feedback can easily be misconstrued as aggressive or harsh. If you have something important to say—such as "Rosie, I really was not happy when I came home, the living room was a mess, there were crackers everywhere, and Olivia never finished her homework"— don't put it in an email or text. If you want your nanny to fully grasp what you are saying, take the time to say it in person.

RULE 6: YOUR NANNY IS NOT A MIND READER

Some parents believe that it is the nanny's responsibility to always know exactly what they need, so they bark orders that are unclear or incomplete and then are furious when the nanny doesn't execute with perfection. I was called in to mediate between one mom and nanny who were in crisis because the mom had screamed at the nanny over a misunderstanding about going to Gymboree. The mom told me, "I was angry because I told her what time the class was, but she wasn't ready to go; she just had the children ready. She ended up needing to change, but I didn't want to be late, so I had to leave her at home and manage the kids all on my own." But the nanny said, "She told me, 'We have Gymboree at 9:30, please have the children ready.' So I got the children changed, I got them into their coats and sneakers, I restocked the diaper bag, and I packed water bottles and snacks. I did everything to get them ready, but she still yelled at me because I wasn't dressed and ready to go. But she never told me that she wanted me to come along!" Your nanny cannot read your mind, and if you don't say something out loud, it may not get done.

Now that we've talked about what *not* to do, let's take a look at how you can communicate your wishes effectively, so that there is no room for misinterpretation or misunderstanding.

How to Direct Your Nanny

The Gold Standard formula for good communication with your nanny is simple: With any statement or request, simply boil it down to its purest form. Take away any emotion and any qualifiers, such as *could* or *would*, and simply state your request in terms of 1-2-3:

1. What you want for your *kids*
2. What you want from your *nanny*
3. What you need for *yourself*

Also, pay close attention not just to *what* you say, but *how* you say it. Whenever you need to direct or correct your nanny, your tone should always be *calm* and *matter of fact*. If you are impatient or condescending or seem like you are annoyed, you will introduce emotion into the situation, and the nanny will not be able to hear you clearly. Instead of focusing on what you are saying, she will focus on how you are making her feel, and if she feels anxious or resentful, there will be tension between you. By speaking in a calm, neutral voice, and clearly stating your needs with the 1-2-3, you don't give her any reason to take it personally or any wiggle room to think that she has a choice or to let her own ideas and needs supplant yours.

For example, in the scenario with the nanny who wasn't ready for Gymboree, instead of yelling at the nanny, the mom should have said:

> We have Gymboree at 9:30. Please have the children dressed and ready with the diaper bag packed, including water bottles and snacks [what you need for your *kids*; it's always better to include specifics like "water bottles," otherwise you might not get them], and please be changed and ready to come with us [what you need from your *nanny*] because I need the extra hands; it's hard for me to manage all three of them on my own [what you need for *yourself*].

Or, if the nanny usually comes along and you'd prefer to go without her, you might say: "I'd like to go to this class alone today. I know you love going, but I really want some bonding time." The idea is to be so direct and straightforward that no one can possibly turn your statement or request into something that it is not.

How to Correct Your Nanny

If you have to address a mistake that your nanny made or bring up an issue that is bothering you, it can sometimes be hard to stick to the Nanny Speak Rules of "clear and straightforward" and "calm and matter of fact." You may struggle to hold your emotions in check, especially if you are upset and concerned about your child. But these are also the times when, no matter how angry you are, it is *most* important to employ the nanny speak technique. It's important to react professionally, rather than emotionally, because doing so will give you the best chance of fixing the mistake and making sure that it doesn't happen again.

Here are some strategies for addressing mistakes effectively with your nanny:

1. CHOOSE YOUR TIMING WISELY

So many parent–nanny conversations go awry because the parent picks a terrible time to bring the issue up—for example, first thing in the morning when everyone is rushing around and the nanny is trying to get the kids fed and off to school, or at the very end of the day when everyone is exhausted and the nanny has to leave to catch her train home. Parents also make the mistake of bringing up issues in the heat of the moment, when they would do better to address them after they've given themselves a chance to calm down and reflect. So before you confront your nanny about something that bothers you, ask yourself:

- **Is there a good reason to bring this up right now?** For example, a safety concern: You're at the playground and you see that your two-year-old is about to try to slide down the fireman's pole, but the nanny is distracted talking to a friend. If it's a genuine issue of safety or an emergency that needs to be addressed immediately, you have every right to bring it up right then and there. If it's not, consider holding your feedback until you and the nanny are both able to focus one-on-one.
- **Is this a teachable moment?** Training your nanny is an ongoing process, so if you have an opportunity to simultaneously correct her and show her how you want something to be done—for example, how your daughter likes her hair fixed or how your son likes his vegetables cut up—it's OK to jump in and take advantage of the moment.
- **Are there other people around?** Nannies, like anyone else, don't want to be reprimanded in front of others. Shaming your nanny or speaking to her in a nasty way in front of other nannies, your friends, or even your spouse or children is embarrassing for her and will almost certainly backfire by making her resentful rather than open to what you are saying.
- **Are you in the right emotional state?** So many mothers have confided to me, "My nanny quit because I was too harsh. If I had just slept on it or cooled down a bit, I would have been able to speak to her about the issue calmly. But I was angry and I yelled, and now she's gone." Unless you need to broach the issue immediately for safety reasons, it's better to step away and reflect and then discuss it when you are in a more rational frame of mind.
- **Who should deliver the message?** If you have a partner or executor nanny, some parents find that it is easier and more effective for the parent who is *not* at home with the nanny most of the time—usually the father—to bring up any issues or problems that need to

be discussed. If it is advantageous for you to have a more friendly relationship with the nanny because you work together all day long, this kind of good cop–bad cop arrangement can make it easier for everyone. If you know from experience that your nanny is more likely to take your feedback seriously when it comes from your partner, hold your commentary until your partner can step in or until you can sit down and address the issue with the nanny together.

If you conclude that the timing isn't right, try to set aside another time to talk to the nanny privately, either in person or over the phone. Maybe you can arrange to come home early one day and put the kids in front of a movie so you can have the conversation. Or perhaps you can bring up the issue during your weekly check-in.

2. STATE YOUR CONCERN, THEN FOLLOW THE NANNY SPEAK FORMULA OF 1-2-3

"Emily, I noticed that you forgot to check Brandon's homework yesterday, and his math was wrong. In the future, please remember to double-check all of his work so he can fix any errors before you place it in the folder." Or "Emily, I saw that you put candy in Jonah's lunch today. The school does not allow candy, so he could get in trouble with his teacher. In the future, please give him a cookie, a brownie, a graham cracker, or a fruit strip instead."

3. IF THE NANNY BECOMES DEFENSIVE, KEEP COOL AND REMIND HER THAT THIS IS BUSINESS

Some nannies will become defensive when faced with any sort of correction or criticism, even if you are presenting your feedback in a calm, rational way. Sometimes this is because they have had bad experiences with former employers and fear that any sort of criticism means they are getting fired; sometimes it is just their personality, and they will automatically try to deflect blame. If this happens, you need to remind the nanny that this is a job and that as the employer, you need to be able to give her feedback—just like a supervisor would in any other profession—so that you can help her do the job better. "Myra, everybody needs to be able to learn on the job, and I understand that everybody makes mistakes. But I need to be able to speak to you openly and honestly about these issues so that you understand what I need from you going forward."

4. IF SHE MAKES EXCUSES, CONCENTRATE ON MOVING FORWARD

Some nannies will make excuse after excuse, trying to justify why they made a mistake or broke your rules. If this happens, don't get caught up in trying to dispute what she says. "I understand, and I'm willing to let it go this time. But we're not going backward, and I don't want to dwell on the past. This is what I need and expect from you going forward."

5. IF IT'S A REPEAT OCCURRENCE, LAY DOWN THE LAW

If your nanny forgot to put sunblock on your child again, and he comes home from camp with another sunburn, you have every right to be upset. Stay calm and do your nanny speak 1-2-3—but then make sure you tell her, "This is now the third time this has happened, and if it happens again, we are going to have a problem, because Charlie was up all night crying from the pain. This is really important, and I don't understand why you aren't listening to me." If it's a serious offense that puts you, your child, or your home at risk, you can tell her that the next time it occurs she will be put on probation or docked pay. This is a last resort, but if the mistake has anything to do with safety, the warning must ring through loud and clear.

Anger Management 101

There is something about the nanny–parent relationship that makes parents, especially mothers, exceedingly judgmental. Perhaps it's because it can be hard to watch someone else doing our job and filling our shoes; we always think that we could do it better. I have met countless mothers who pick, pick, pick at their nanny all day long over minor things or yell at their nannies over every little mistake. I have seen mothers become so furious that they slam doors or throw things at the nanny—shoes, clothes, and once even a laptop computer!

CORRECTING MISTAKES: WHAT YOUR NANNY IS THINKING

Whenever you bring up any issue with your nanny, her first thought will likely be, "Am I getting fired?" It is this fear, along with the fear of losing income, that pushes many nannies to make excuses and become defensive, even if you are using good nanny speak and presenting the problem in a calm, rational way. If the nanny starts getting upset, it can help to come right out and reassure her, "Look, we really like having you here, and this doesn't mean that we want you to leave. I just want to discuss it with you so that we can make sure it doesn't happen again." Once that fear and distraction is removed from her mind, she will be able to focus and listen.

It can be easy, in the heat of the moment, to suddenly lose control and act inappropriately because you're upset, and you're in your home and no one is watching. There's no supervisory board that will hold you accountable and no coworkers to raise their eyebrows if you lose your cool. But *you* need to hold yourself accountable because you are an employer, and you need to act professionally, if not just for your nanny, then for the sake of your children. If you treat your nanny poorly, and humiliate her and wear her down, she is going to be resentful, and she won't give her best to your child. Here are some tips to help you keep your emotions under control:

- **Ask yourself, "Do I have a right to be angry?"** You only have a right to be angry and express your anger if it is over something that the nanny should have known—for example, if it is a basic childcare or safety issue that is *not specific to your home*, such as never leaving a baby alone in the bathtub. If it is something specific to your household and the particular way you want things done—for example, putting bug spray on the children every time they go outside—and if you haven't told her about it directly, then the blame lies with you, not her.
- **Challenge any unkind, irrational thoughts.** If you react emotionally, and think, "Wendy forgot the snacks, my God she is so stupid!" those words may fly out of your mouth when you confront the nanny. Before you say something you'll regret, take a deep breath and challenge your thoughts: "Is Wendy really stupid? Well no, not really. She has a college degree and has worked well here for two years. She just forgets things when I don't write them down."
- **Pretend that you are in an office environment.** Before you lay into her, ask yourself: If you were in a professional setting, would you be acting this way right now? How would you speak to your employee if you worked in a bank? I've had clients fire back, "But

THE POWER OF NEGATIVE THINKING

We are all occasionally prone to angry, irrational thoughts, but a pattern of negative thinking can hurt your relationship with your nanny and prevent you from interacting in a positive way. Here are some thought patterns that can lead to trouble:

- **Seeing the situation as black and white.** Moms tend to think that the nanny is either *great* or *terrible*, but everyone has shades of gray. No nanny is perfect.
- **Personalizing.** This happens when you make the nanny's mistakes about you—"She does not respect me and won't listen"—rather than just seeing them for what they are.
- **Mind reading.** "I know that when she is quiet, she is angry about something that I asked her to do." Instead of reading the nanny's mind and assuming the worst, be up front about it, and just ask her what she is thinking.
- **Catastrophizing.** So many mothers think the world is ending over small events. I had a mother call me crying hysterically because her nanny had asked if she could work five days a week rather than six. She thought that the nanny asking for weekends off meant that she did not care about them or their child and wanted to leave. What was the truth? I talked to the nanny and she told me, "I love this family and will never leave them, but I made a lot of nice friends this past year, and I'd like to have weekends off." That was it. Two years later, everything is fine, the nanny got the extra day off, and it was all much ado about nothing.
- **Overgeneralizing.** "Terri always messes up..." "Susan never listens to me..." I hear parents say these things all the time. If the nanny truly *always* makes mistakes or *never* listens, then you should fire her. But if you overgeneralize that she is bad and focus on her mistakes rather than her successes, you may talk yourself out of appreciating a perfectly good nanny. As in any situation, you will do better to focus on the positives.

this isn't a bank, it's my house!" It doesn't matter. As an employer, you must *always* speak to your nanny the way you would speak to any other employee. If you don't, you are falling down on your duty as a boss.

- **Weigh the mistake in light of the nanny's pros and cons.** Everyone makes mistakes, so you need to view each incident in light of the nanny's performance on the whole. Ask yourself, "Even with this mistake, do the nanny's pros far outweigh her cons?" If the answer is yes, then don't make a big deal out of the event.

When Your Nanny Approaches You

If your nanny approaches you about an issue or problem that she is having, you should know first and foremost that it's a *good* thing. If she cares about you and the job enough to want to sit down and discuss what's bothering her, you know that you have someone who values your relationship and wants to be proactive about making it work. That said, just as nannies can become defensive, parents can become defensive as well. It's easy and even natural to feel annoyed and think, "Who are you to be telling me what to do with my kids in my house?" But if you are going to employ someone in your home, you need to be open to hearing about how they can work best for you. Whatever your nanny brings to you, you want to make sure that you react professionally and that your response mirrors what you would expect from her. Here are some tips for keeping your cool as a boss and responding to your nanny in a productive way:

- **Make sure that you are ready to hear her.** If it's not a good time, if you're rushed or distracted, let her know, but don't walk away without agreeing on another time to talk.
- **Listen** to what she has to say. Hear her out, and don't interrupt.

- **Validate her feelings.** "I understand that this bothered you, and I'm sorry that you're upset."
- **Don't try to win.** If you disagree, you can explain your side of the story, but don't get caught up in a lot of back and forth and don't try to convince the nanny that you are right. Whoever is right or

---

THE NANNY RULE OF TENS

When I do couples therapy, I always make the clients promise that they will speak about a problem when their annoyance or frustration reaches an "anger level" of two or three, rather than waiting and exploding at level ten. When you hit level ten, you run the risk of ruining or severing the relationship, and you may reach the point of thinking, "There is no possible way to fix this, and it needs to end."

Unfortunately, nannies almost *always* wait to speak about something that bothers them until they hit a level ten inside. This is why you hear countless stories from parents who say, "My nanny just up and quit" or "My nanny just didn't show up on Monday" or "When we came home from our trip, the nanny was all packed up and gone." Nannies in general do not feel comfortable voicing their feelings or frustrations to their employers, so they wait and wait until they hit their breaking point. But given that many married couples have trouble speaking up at a level of two or three, it's not surprising that nannies struggle with this as well.

You can prevent this from happening by telling your nanny at the outset that you want her to be honest and that it is OK if she comes to you with any problems or concerns about the job. You can say, "I really want you to be happy here, and we hope to be together for a long time. If there is anything that is bothering you or isn't working for you, please tell me so that we can figure out how to make it better."

wrong or who did what to whom is beside the point. The real question is, How can you make sure it doesn't happen again?

- **Collaborate on a solution.** Ask the nanny for her thoughts on how you can improve the situation and share your ideas as well. If a problem is truly intractable, you may need to reevaluate whether you and the nanny can work together. If you are unwilling to make changes or agree on a solution, you need to recognize that your nanny may quit.
- **Move on.** Once it's over, let it go, and don't hold a grudge. Grudges are a killer for any nanny–parent relationship.

If You Sense That Something Is Wrong

Sometimes the nanny won't approach you about a problem, but you can tell by the way she's acting that something is bothering her. In these cases, it is extremely important to approach your nanny as soon as possible and give her an opening to talk, rather than to just stand by. In most other professions, maintaining personal privacy and keeping your frustrations to yourself is acceptable and even advisable. But when someone is working in your home and around your children, you need to know what's going on in her mind in real time.

In these cases, you want to wait for the right moment, and then say, "Joanna, you seem a little upset today. You're very quiet. Is something bothering you?" or "Joanna, you didn't say much when you left yesterday, and you don't seem like your usual self. Is everything all right?" If she is not forthcoming, you should always follow up with, "If there's anything that I have done, please let me know. I want you to tell me so that we can talk about it, clear the air, and move on." If she talks, you will need to stand by your word and be receptive to what she says and not get defensive or dwell on it. If she says, "I was really embarrassed yesterday when your friend was here; you were very short with me and demanded that I bring you things. I felt like I was a servant rather than a nanny." Even if there is nothing you can do to fix the situation, simply saying "I'm sorry" will go a long way.

If your nanny is really acting strangely—if she seems notably stressed or agitated, or if there has been a real change from her baseline personality—*don't* just keep quiet and let it go. We'll talk more about strange or erratic behavior and how to handle it in Chapter 10.

Communicating with your nanny can be uniquely complex because even though on paper you are employer and employee, in reality you are bonded together in the most personal of ways: by sharing each other's space and by a mutual deep caring and responsibility for your child. In Chapter 11, we'll take a closer look at the relationship between mothers and nannies, and at the many different emotions that come into play when there's another woman in the house.

CHAPTER 10

———•———

Troubleshooting

Nanny Whisperer Strategies for Fixing
Common Problems

No nanny–family relationship is ever perfect, and even when a nanny has been with you for many years, there will always be new issues that crop up. Most of these can be smoothed over by working together as partners, keeping up with your training forms, and using the nanny speak techniques in Chapter 9. But every now and then you may be faced with a larger issue that needs special handling or even calls the entire relationship into question—and that's what this chapter is about.

The truth is that as hard as you have worked to screen your nanny, *any* nanny—no matter how wonderful she is with your child or how long she has worked for you—is capable of having a lapse in judgment. Sometimes there is an issue in the nanny's personal life that causes her to become distracted or irresponsible; sometimes the line between family member and employee becomes so blurred that the nanny gets too comfortable and behaves in an unprofessional manner. And the blurrier that line gets, the harder it can be to confront your nanny and take a stand when something is unacceptable. If the nanny loves your child, and he loves her, the idea of possibly losing her care and having to start all over again can seem like too big a risk to take.

> At the end of the day, this is about your child.

As the employer, however, you have every right to demand that your nanny provide a high-quality level of care and that she respect your wishes because that's what you are paying her to do. It can be tempting to look the other way and pretend that the issue doesn't exist, but I strongly urge you not to do so because at the end of the day, this is about your child.

Your job as a parent, first and foremost, is to ensure that your child is happy and safe and that he is getting what he needs—physically, developmentally, and emotionally—whenever you are not there. Your job as an employer is to hold your employee accountable for any actions or mistakes that suggest a lack of effort or disregard for your

---

NANNY CAMS: SHOULD YOU USE ONE?

If you are thinking about using a nanny cam, it is essential that you inform the nanny. You don't have to ask her permission because legally you are allowed to video anyone in your own home. But if you *don't* tell the nanny, and then need to confront her about something you've seen, you will be in the very awkward position of having to explain that you've been videoing her without her knowledge. That kind of deception can really undermine the trust in your relationship, so I strongly advise you to be honest about it from the start. Most good nannies won't have an issue with it because they know they have nothing to hide.

The easiest way to explain that you'll be using a nanny cam is to tell the nanny that it has nothing to do with her and more to do with you being able to see your child and know what he is doing every day. You can say, "It's very hard for us to be away from our son, we really miss him when we're at work, so it's helpful for us to log on during the day and see that he is safe and happy." Make sure to reiterate that this is not about your trust or confidence in her but more about feeling connected to your child.

---

rules and authority. Sometimes the larger problems that arise with a nanny are fixable and forgivable, and sometimes they're not. Here is a guide to thinking through the most common issues and deciding what kind of impact they should have on your relationship.

Accidents

If your child gets hurt on the nanny's watch, your first emotional response will be to get angry and blame the nanny. Once I asked Maria to place Braydin in her walker, shut the door to the basement, and come meet me in the kitchen. Well, Maria forgot to shut the door and my little lady went flying down the stairs. I was furious—but five minutes later when Braydin was laughing at Barney and we realized that she was totally fine, we both burst out crying, and I saw in her face the genuine pain and concern she felt about what had occurred. I thought about what to do and realized that accidents happen to children all the time, even when they are under their parents' care. All of us get tired and distracted by our various responsibilities and any of us can make a mistake. As long as the nanny is honest with you about what happened and doesn't try to cover it up, and as long as she has proved herself to be otherwise attentive and responsible, it is worth keeping her and trying again. Instead of focusing on blaming and shaming your nanny, the best thing to do is focus on training and how to prevent the accident from reoccurring. After Braydin's fall, we installed a baby gate inside the basement door for added protection and stepped up our other baby-proofing measures throughout the house.

If the accident caused your child to have a serious injury and was due to an act of extreme negligence—such as leaving the gate to the pool unlatched or allowing your child to run into the street—your trust in the nanny may be irreparably shattered, even if she wasn't directly at fault. If this is the case, and you just can't view the situation from a more rational perspective and get past it, I believe that it's better to start fresh with someone new.

Blurred Boundaries

Some parents feel completely comfortable treating the nanny as part of their family, while others prefer a more professional relationship. The boundaries between family member and employee are most likely to become blurred in a live-in situation, but there are also occasionally live-out nannies who, either intentionally or unintentionally, cross the line. I remember after we first hired Maria, when I was lying in bed cuddling with my middle daughter, Presley, and Maria came up the stairs singing, "Where's my baby?" Presley heard her and called, "Mimi, Mimi!" and Maria came in and literally scooped her out of my arms. There were moments when, as much as I loved Maria, I just didn't want to share my home or family, or special moments with the girls, with her. It took some time, but eventually I learned how to be strong enough to come right out and tell her what I needed when I became uncomfortable or felt like our family needed space.

If you feel that your nanny has gotten too close for comfort and that it is starting to affect you personally (for example, you feel like you never have any private time with your spouse or kids) or impinge on how you run your household (the nanny starts feeling a bit too comfortable and isn't doing what she's told), then you will have to speak up and draw the line, even if it's touchy. When you want privacy, ask for privacy: "Janice, I'd like to talk to Tommy alone," or "We'd really like to have the evenings after dinner be family time. You're welcome to eat with us, but then I'd like you to head upstairs to your room." Be sure that you tangibly state what the problem is because simply saying "We feel like the lines have gotten blurry" won't be clear. Instead, make a list of the things that bother you—such as "She sits down to read the paper with us at the end of the night"—and then figure out how you can direct the nanny to correct them.

Child Doesn't Like the Nanny

Sometimes a child just doesn't like a nanny, and if this happens, you will need to play detective and try to figure out why. If your child is older, it may take him a while to warm up to a new nanny, and this is completely normal. You should start by doing your best to facilitate bonding by giving the nanny fun things to do with your child, and telling the nanny how to best engage him (see the strategies in Chapter 8).

If your child seems truly unhappy or anxious in a way that is clearly out of character, then you will need to closely monitor the situation. Children can be barometers, so never dismiss their feelings outright. Sometimes using a nanny cam is the only way to know the absolute truth, or if you can, try spending more time with the nanny and child at home. If you stay home and you see that the nanny is trying everything, that she's following all of your suggestions but it just isn't working, it may be that it's not a good personality match. Some children from the age of eighteen months and up can experience severe stranger anxiety, in which case anyone who isn't Mom or Dad may elicit the same response. To test whether you are dealing with a general attachment issue or a problem with a particular nanny, start trialing other caregivers or having other babysitters around. If your child is consistently upset by anyone new in the house, the problem is most likely not with your nanny per se. If you're a working mom, you can also see if your child does better in daycare. Usually these situations do improve, but you should do whatever you can to spend time with your nanny and child until it does.

If it seems that your child is routinely upset by one particular person, then unless that person is of crucial necessity, you don't want to have her in your home. This doesn't mean it's the nanny's fault; it just means that for whatever reason—and with preverbal children you may never know the reason—the child experiences some sort of anxiety whenever that person is present. If you have tried to help the situation but it is still not working, you should end the relationship, and when you start your search for someone new, make sure that you do multiple, full-day trials.

Favoritism

If you have multiple children, it is possible that your nanny may show a preference for one particular child, especially if she has raised that child from infancy, but not the others. There will almost always be a closer bond between the nanny and any child that she has cared for since birth, and usually that child will also be the one who loves and respects the nanny more, which only perpetuates the nanny's prefer-ence. I have seen cases where the nanny would read three books to one child and none to the other or kiss and hug one child all the time but rarely show affection to her siblings. This kind of favoritism can be very demoralizing to the child who is *not* the apple of the nanny's eye, so if this happens in your family, you need to step up as a parent and help the nanny close the gap.

The first step is to sit the nanny down and have a frank, non-emotional conversation about the situation. Try to frame it as a discussion about job performance and helping the nanny to balance her

---

TEARS WHEN YOU LEAVE: IS IT THE NANNY'S FAULT?

If you are a working mom, and your child cries every time the nanny shows up, don't necessarily take it as a sign that the nanny isn't doing a good job. Even very young children of working parents can make the connection that "when this lady shows up, Mommy leaves," and this can be understandably scary. Usually the situation will resolve in time, but if you're really worried, you can put in cameras and see what's happening when you're not there (see "Nanny Cams: Should You Use One?" on page 200). In nine out of ten cases, the child is fine as soon as the mother leaves—it's just the transition and the moment of departure that cause stress.

On the flip side, I have also seen children who cry and act out as soon as the mother gets home. Again, this usually has nothing to do with the nanny and is more about the child seeking attention from the parent. It can be easy to ask, "What has been going on here all day that has my child so distraught?" but the likelihood is that your child was fine during the day and now just wants the reassurance of having Mom comfort and coddle him a little. If you're unsure, having a family member or friend drop by unannounced during the day or using a nanny cam can help allay your fears. Remember that no matter how good your nanny is, your children love you more than anything, so it is natural that they will put up a fight when you leave or clamor for your attention the moment you return.

---

responsibilities. You can say, "Right now, the care between the children, and the attention you give them are split eighty–twenty, and we need it to be split fifty–fifty. How can we achieve that?" You also need to provide tangible examples of what you would like the nanny to do differently because you can't just say, "I want you to care for them both the same." Realistically that may not be possible, but the level of interaction, attention, and physical affection needs to be equal, and you need to be able to tell the nanny what that looks like: "If Sam and Bella do not want to play together, you need to take turns letting each one choose the activity and playing with them separately for a short while if need be. You could also try to engage them in a board game—usually they will both join in for that." Sometimes one child (usually the older one) may actually resist closeness, and the nanny may say, "I try to give him hugs but he runs away" or "She doesn't listen to me; she slams her door." If this is the case, you will need to be proactive and think of ways to help the nanny develop a relationship with that child.

Because developing relationships takes time, I usually recommend that parents give the nanny at least a month to try to improve the situation. If nothing changes, it may be necessary to let the nanny go and start fresh with someone who can come in and care for your children equally.

Disregard for Your Work Agreement or Household Rules

If you and the nanny have a written Nanny–Family Work Agreement in place (see page 147) that you both signed when she accepted and started the job, and you are well beyond the initial training phase, there is no excuse for breaking the rules or failing to perform the duties you initially laid out for her. Some examples would be using a cell phone around your child when you expressly stated that it was one of your Deal-Breakers or failing to do the dishes or prepare bottles every day if you listed these in the job description as some of your Musts. If she is not upholding her end of the agreement, you can be a bit tougher than you would normally be in a straight nanny speak correct-and-redirect conversation. Here is what you should do:

1. **Arrange a time to speak with the nanny** about her actions (or inaction) as soon as possible.

2. **State what happened** in a calm, non-emotional manner: "You failed to do the dishes on three different days this week, and forgot to prepare the bottles almost every night." If appropriate, add: "You know that we expect you to do these things every day, because they are in our work agreement."

3. **Ask,** "Is there something going on that is affecting your job that we should know about?" and give the nanny a chance to explain.

4. **If there is a reasonable explanation** (family troubles, health issues, emotional news) and the nanny seems remorseful, ask her, "How do you think you can work while you are going through this?" Maybe she needs a personal day, or perhaps she will feel better by simply having told you.

   Then make a plan. Discuss what you expect from her during this time, and/or an appropriate time frame for getting back to normal. "OK, now that I understand what happened, let's see how you do next week, and let me know if there's a problem."

5. **If the nanny becomes angry or defensive,** remain calm and state, "Your tone seems very angry right now. Is there something that is upsetting you that you would like to address? This is not what we agreed to, so I'm simply trying to understand what's going on."

6. **If she makes excuses that do not seem reasonable**—and keep in mind that only rarely is there a reasonable explanation for

neglecting basic duties or breaking your rules—you can say, "I'm not interested in looking backward. Going forward, I need you to do the dishes and prepare the bottles every day, because that's what we originally agreed to, and that's what we need for this job."

7. **If she says that she can't do what is being asked,** you will need to decide if her reasoning makes sense and if you can live without the task you are requesting. If you can't, then you will have to say, "I'm a working mom, and I really need someone to do the dishes and tidy up the kitchen before I come home. If you cannot do these things, then this may not be the right position for you."

If you do *not* have a Nanny–Family Work Agreement in place, you should create one as soon as possible using the guidelines in Chapter 7. You can then present it to the nanny and say, "Since there has been some confusion about our rules and/or what we need, we thought it would be helpful to outline everything on paper. We can both sign it, and then you will have this agreement to refer to if anything is unclear going forward."

You Need More Help Than You Originally Thought

This scenario is very common with first-time parents who have never had a nanny before, or who go through the hiring process without doing a thorough Family Needs Assessment and using my FNA form (see Chapter 3). As we've said, it can be extremely hard to change the rules of the game and tack on additional duties after your nanny starts, and asking her to do more than she initially agreed to can breed frustration and bad feelings between you. That said, almost every job evolves over time, so you may be able to change the job parameters if you do so respectfully and, most important, at the right time.

The best strategy is to raise the issue during a formal review or on an anniversary—for example, when the nanny has been with you for six months or a year. You can say, "We're really happy with the way things are going, but every job changes over time, and now that you've been with us for a year, we'd like to talk about modifying your responsibilities. There are some things that we feel we really need our nanny to do that, as first-time parents, we didn't know we needed when we hired you." You should then outline exactly which duties you'd like her to take on, and be prepared to explain how you envision her fitting them into her day ("We feel that there is plenty of time to do some additional laundry and use the Swiffer while Dylan naps"). If the nanny agrees, be sure to update your training forms and Work Agreement so that the new duties are spelled out clearly.

Be forewarned, however, that the nanny may very well respond by saying, "This isn't the job I agreed to do, and I already have my hands full doing X, Y, Z," or "I'd be happy to do these things, but I'll need more money," especially if the new duties are not child related. These responses are perfectly legitimate, and you will need to decide how to respond based on your own situation. If your current nanny is unwilling to meet your changing needs, and you can't outsource the additional duties to a cleaning person or a second childcare provider such as a babysitter, then it may be better for everyone if you find someone else who is capable of meeting the revised parameters of the job. Parents who are paying good money for a nanny should never feel stressed and overwhelmed because they aren't getting what they need on the home front.

Slacking Off

Sometimes a nanny will start letting things slide once she gets comfortable or has been with your family for a few years. Suddenly the kids are watching more TV, the laundry is getting done only every other day, and she no longer goes the extra mile to make sure that the house is neat and tidy when you come home. If the nanny has always been terrific up to this point, you may feel like you want to give her the benefit of the doubt and avoid saying anything that will rock the boat. But in my experience, slacking off is a slippery slope. There are nannies who will test the waters to see what they can get away with, and if they skip the laundry a couple of times and no one says anything, they will conclude—correctly—that they can get away with it. Confronting a nanny about what you've noticed right away is the best, most effective way to keep her on her toes, so if you see any signs that your nanny is going off track, you owe it to yourself and your child to nip it in the bud.

Here is how to approach your nanny:

1. **State** what she is doing well.
2. **Explain** that you want the relationship to continue for a long time, and that you want to address something that has come up so that you can understand what happened and work it out. Reassure her that she is not being fired so that she will not be distracted.
3. **Ask,** "Are the duties that we've given you too overwhelming? Because you used to be able to do X and Y, but now I have noticed that X and Y are not done."

THE LITMUS TEST FOR BAD BEHAVIOR

If you are trying to figure out whether your nanny's actions are excusable, ask yourself: "Would this be a problem at another job?" Anything that would be professionally unacceptable in a regular workplace should be unacceptable in your home as well.

---

4. **If she says, "Yes, this is too much for me,"** then you need to think, "Is this a reasonable statement?"

- If it *is* reasonable—for example, you've had a second child and now she is caring for an infant as well as managing all of her former responsibilities—then perhaps the workload is too much. If you want to keep her, you will need to adjust.
- If it is *not* reasonable, then you need to say, "I'm sorry that you feel that way, but we believe that there is plenty of time during naptime to get these things done as well as take some time for yourself, and we need them to be done for this job."

Attitude

In the same way that parents can sometimes be rude or short with their nannies, nannies can also be rude or short with parents. Some nannies will have a chip on their shoulder and be sulky, snippy, or defensive from the moment you hire them; others may develop an attitude problem if they feel that they are being mistreated or disrespected. If you've been through my Gold Standard hiring process, you have, I hope, avoided the ones with an attitude problem that can't be fixed. However, I've also seen plenty of situations where the nanny had good cause for an attitude problem because her employers treated her so unfairly. If you scream and curse at your nanny or call her stupid and speak to her in a way that is completely unprofessional, or if you pile on additional responsibilities and run her ragged into the ground, your nanny has every right to be upset. So if your nanny is suddenly giving you an attitude, you need to first ask why and then be open to hearing the answer. Here's how to address it:

1. **Ask, "Have we done something to upset you?** Because I notice that you seem unhappy. You were very short with me just now

when I asked you about the day's schedule. We want you to be happy here, so I would rather you be honest and tell me so that I can see if there is a way to fix it."

2. **If there is a good reason**—for example, you've been asking her to do tasks that weren't in the original job description—then you will need to acknowledge that she has a point and try to rectify the situation.

3. **If there is not a good reason,** then you can put her on notice: "We need the attitude to resolve immediately for us to continue working together. Can you do this? If not, this may not be the right job for you." Give her a week; if the attitude persists, you should let her go and find someone else.

Lying

Lying from your nanny can be a difficult pill to swallow because, usually, where there's one lie, there's more. That said, not all lies are equal. There are little lies, big lies, and medium lies that fall in between, and I've seen situations where the parents fired the nanny right away as well as situations where the parents were able to get past it and work it out. If you catch your nanny in a lie, your challenge as an employer is to think it through and figure out: How important is this lie? Does it indicate a significant character flaw or lapse in judgment? And most important, should it be a cause for termination?

To help you understand how to think about these questions, let's look at three different examples from three moms who sought my guidance. The first mom, Kendra, caught her nanny lying while she was talking to her on the phone. She had called her nanny from work to see how the day was going, and while she was talking to the nanny, she logged on to her nanny cam from her work computer and could see that her son was awake in his crib and babbling. So she asked the nanny, "Is he up yet?" and the nanny answered, "No, he's still asleep." But Kendra knew that the nanny would have been able to hear her son and see him on the monitor, so she had lied to cover up the fact that she hadn't gone in to pick him up.

The second mom, Stephanie, caught her nanny lying when she reviewed the video footage on her nanny cam. Stephanie and her husband were both musicians, and they had been concerned that their nanny wasn't playing enough music for their son. So they had asked her to play at least two CDs a day, one of which was supposed to be classical music, and to write down which CDs she played in their daily log. The nanny had agreed, but when Stephanie watched the footage after a few weeks had gone by, she realized that the nanny wasn't actually playing the music at all—she was just writing down the names of a few CDs every day. Stephanie was stunned because not only had the nanny disobeyed their wishes, but she had also lied—in writing—to make it seem as if she were following through.

The third mom, Lydia, had had the same nanny for four years, and the whole family loved her and the situation was very positive. Lydia and her husband both worked full-time, so they kept the nanny even after their youngest child started elementary school. Over the course of a few months, they noticed that the mileage on their car was up, and they questioned the nanny about it: "Have you been driving the car outside our neighborhood?" The nanny assured them that she wasn't, but the mileage kept getting higher, so they finally installed a GPS tracker and discovered that the nanny had been driving the car home every day. She would drop the children off at school, drive twenty miles to her house, spend six hours at home, and then drive back to school in time to pick the children up. Not only had she lied about taking the car but she had been twenty miles away every day when Lydia and her husband were paying her to take care of their home and be on-call for their kids.

Now let's take a look at how to assess each situation, and how to decide whether the lie presents a significant problem.

WEIGHING THE LIE

Whenever you're trying to decide whether or not a nanny's lie should be a big deal, you should ask yourself the following questions:

1. Is There Anything Reasonable About the Lie That You Can Understand?

First, put yourself in the nanny's shoes and try to see where she was coming from. In the case of Kendra and her nanny, think about what you would have done in the same situation: The baby just woke up, but your boss is calling—do you go get the baby or take the call? You would probably decide to take the call first, otherwise your boss will wonder where you are. But then when your boss asks you if the baby is up, you don't want her to think that you're neglecting her child, so you lie and say, "Oh no, he's not up yet." Yes, it's a lie, but you can understand how the nanny might have felt boxed in and lied for the sake of keeping her boss happy and that it is most likely an isolated incident. The child was awake, but he was safe and happy in his crib, so there was no real harm done.

In the cases of Stephanie and Lydia, however, it is much harder to understand where the nanny was coming from. Would you ever willfully opt *not to do* something that your boss asked you to do, especially when it was something as simple as playing music for a child? Would you ever take someone's vehicle against his or her wishes and spend the day at home when you were being paid to be somewhere else? In both of these cases, there was nothing reasonable or explainable about the nannies' actions.

2. Was the Lie Premeditated?

In the case of Kendra's nanny, it was a lie on the fly—a lie that the nanny spontaneously told in response to a specific situation. She was put on the spot, and she didn't want to get into trouble. But in Stephanie and Lydia's cases, the lie was premeditated. These nannies *deliberately chose* to take a course of action that was against their employers' wishes. Stephanie's nanny agreed to play the CDs and then actually wrote them down on a list even when she didn't do it. Lydia's nanny continued to take the car even after the parents questioned her and reiterated that it was not allowed. It goes without saying that a premeditated lie is much more serious that a spontaneous one because it indicates that the nanny actually put thought into the decision, and still chose an act of willful deception.

3. Is There a Pattern of Deception?

In the case of Kendra's nanny, there was nothing to suggest that the lie was anything other than a one-time event that resulted from a specific situation. The nanny had been doing a terrific job for more than a year, and Kendra had never seen anything else on the nanny cam that caused her concern or alarm. But in Stephanie and Lydia's case, the nannies had lied again and again over a period of weeks. Anyone can lie once in a blue moon to save face, but if someone is lying to you on a regular basis about anything—large or small—it indicates a character flaw that you do not want in your child's caregiver.

4. Were Your Needs or Your Child's Needs
Significantly Compromised in Any Way?

Your nanny's number one job is to care for your child, and her number two job is to make your life easier. So if by lying she is falling down on her responsibilities and ignoring your Musts, not only is she being dishonest but she's also not doing her job. In Kendra's case, her nanny's lie did *not* significantly compromise her child's needs; yes, maybe the nanny could have gotten to him sooner, but the child was fine and safe until she did. In Stephanie's case, the nanny's lie did not endanger the child, but it directly compromised what Stephanie and her husband felt was an important developmental need for their son. In Lydia's case, the nanny's deception significantly compromised both the needs of the parents—because she wasn't home taking care of the house—and more important, those of the children, because if there had ever been an emergency that required her to get them quickly, she would have been unavailable. This question and the degree to which your needs have been compromised and whether or not your child was endangered are what should tip the scales if you are on the fence about whether to fire or not to fire.

In general, if you answered yes to question 1—meaning that there could be a reasonable explanation for why the nanny lied—and you care about the relationship (Kendra's case), you should have a frank conversation with the nanny to address the issue, clear the air, and make sure that you are on the same page about the need for absolute honesty. If you answered no to question 1 and yes to one or two of the other questions (Stephanie's case), but you still want to try to salvage the relationship, you will need to have a much more stern conversation in which you inform the nanny that she is on thin ice. If you answered no to question 1 and yes to *all* of the other questions (Lydia's case), I strongly advise you to end the relationship.

CONFRONTING THE NANNY

Whether it's a big lie or a little lie, you should *never let a lie go unaddressed*. By sweeping it under the rug, you set the stage for future lying as well as a lack of trust in your relationship. By addressing it up front, you have a chance to get back on track. The severity of the lie, and how you feel about the nanny on the whole, will determine how you should approach the conversation.

The Little Lie (Kendra's Case)

If you want the relationship with your nanny to continue and also to avoid future lies, you have to give her a safe space to open up so that she can be honest about what happened and you can work through it together. Here's how to do it:

1. **Reassure her.** "I really like you and I want our relationship to continue, but I want to talk to you about something."
2. **State what happened.** "The other day when I called you, I asked if the baby was up yet, and you said no. But I saw on my camera at work that the baby was awake."
3. **Explain.** "I just want to know why you did that, and if there is anything I have done to make you feel that you cannot be honest with me." Then listen to what she says.
4. **Tell her what you want.** "We need complete honesty for this relationship to work, so in the future, I want you to feel comfortable saying, 'Yes, he's up, but I took your call first.' I would rather you tell me the truth."
5. **Let her know the consequences of lying going forward.** "I understand that everyone makes mistakes, but we expect complete honesty from now on. If this happens again, we won't be able to work together."

If you have been through my process and have lying or dishonesty listed under "Grounds for Immediate Termination" in your Nanny–Family Work Agreement, be sure to remind the nanny of what she signed when she started the job.

The Medium Lie (Stephanie's Case)

Stephanie's situation was tricky because her nanny's lie fell in the gray area between "not so bad" and "fireable." On the one hand, they had always been happy with the nanny and the lie didn't pose any great risk to their son. On the other hand, it was a deliberate lie that occurred multiple times and went directly against their wishes.

In a situation like this, you need to be extremely firm and clear about what you expect from the nanny as your employee. Here is how to do so effectively:

- **Don't feel like you need to reassure her** ("We really like you and we really want this to work") because you want her to know that you mean business and that her job is on the line.
- **Instead, be direct.** "We know that you have been lying to us about the CDs, because we saw you on the cameras writing down CDs that you never played."
- **Put her on notice.** "We're not interested in excuses, and we want to make it absolutely clear that from this point on, lying about anything—whether it's a big thing like an accident that harmed our child or something as little as what he wore that day—is grounds for immediate termination."

Even if the nanny is appropriately contrite, you may want to start to look for a new nanny anyway, because a caregiver who lies repeatedly is not someone you want watching your child.

The Big Lie (Lydia's Case)

If the lie is serious enough that it has put your child in danger, or is such a betrayal of trust that you severely question the nanny's judgment and ability to do her job, I recommend that you terminate the relationship immediately (see Chapter 12).

Stealing

Unlike lying, which may be a harmless one-time act, stealing is a direct sign that something is amiss. Before you jump to conclusions, however, you need to consider the item in question. I had one mother call me up screaming because the nanny had stolen shampoo. When I questioned the nanny, she said, "It was in my shower, so I took it home for the weekend." Similar situations often arise over food if the nanny mistakenly takes something from the fridge that isn't hers. For smaller, less consequential items, you want to make sure that the nanny didn't take them due to a genuine misunderstanding.

If you believe that your nanny has been stealing, you need to tread very, very lightly. First, you need to ask yourself, "How sure am I?" and "Do I have definite proof?" If you don't have proof, is there a way to get it so that you are absolutely sure? I had one mother who'd had money go missing from her purse on several occasions, so the next time she went to the cash machine, she marked all the bills. When her money went missing again, she found the marked bills in the nanny's bag.

If you feel that you have proof, or enough circumstantial evidence that you would rather not continue to have the nanny in your home, you should immediately move to end the relationship. You can choose whether or not to confront the nanny about the stealing, but I generally believe that in these situations, the less that is said, and the more

calmly you can part ways, the better. If the stealing is especially serious or involves a big-ticket item like an expensive piece of jewelry, you
can notify the police, remove your children from the home, and let
the authorities handle the rest.

Strange or Erratic Behavior

Any time you notice a disturbing change in your nanny's behavior,
you need to address it right away. Sadly, I have known cases where the
nanny did make errors that put the children at risk, and when I questioned the parents, they noted that she had been acting "differently."
These differences might manifest in personality changes (more quiet,
more agitated, seeming anxious or distracted, becoming angry, or
losing patience) or changes in her appearance (weight loss, weight
gain, poor hygiene, or looking particularly tired or worn out). If your
nanny is left alone with your children, and you notice any of these
signs, you should arrange to speak to the nanny as soon as possible to
make sure that she is mentally able to handle your children and the
pressures of the job. You can say, "I've noticed that you are not yourself lately. You seem [angry, anxious, nervous, forgetful]. Is there
something going on that you would like to tell us about?"

- **If she gives a reason that is logical and fixable**—for example, "I've
  just been worried about my son; he is getting a divorce" or "My
  arthritis has really been bothering me"—and she seems safe to
  handle the children, you can keep a watchful eye to make sure that
  the situation is improving and she is getting help.
- **If she gives a reason that is logical but not fixable**—she is going
  through a divorce, a family member has a drug problem, a sudden
  job loss is creating stress and putting the family in debt—you
  should tell the nanny that you empathize with what she's going

through, and if you want to, offer her help. I know plenty of families who have helped their nannies through hard times after a spouse lost his job either by paying salary up front or adding hours. If you are unable to help, and the situation is still causing the nanny major stress, then you need to frankly say, "We need to know that you are OK and stable enough to be able to do the job. Do you feel that you can focus enough to continue working here?" If she says yes, give it a week and see how she does. If the behavior doesn't change, then you will need to seriously think about replacement.

- **If it's medically related**—such as side effects from a medication or issues pertaining to mental health—then you may need to give her a leave of absence, especially if she is a parental unit nanny who takes care of the children alone. If she is a partner or executor nanny and one parent is always home, then you may choose to have her continue while you keep a close watch.
- **If the nanny will not disclose the reason,** but you know in your gut that something is off, the best course of action is to have her take a leave of absence, while you find backup and start the search for a new nanny.

SHOULD YOU EVER DO PROBATION?

I don't endorse doing the "official" threat probation—that is, telling the nanny, "You're on probation for the next two weeks and if things don't change we can't continue" because in my experience, the minute a nanny thinks that she's getting fired, she will be halfway out the door. If you want to give the nanny a chance to improve, the best thing to do is have a probationary period in your mind and tell yourself, "I'm going to give it two weeks and if it doesn't get better, I'll start looking for someone else."

In my experience, too many parents are reluctant to give their nannies time off to deal with personal problems, but I feel that this is a huge mistake. If your nanny is overwhelmed by something that is happening in her personal life and she can't leave her problems at the door, as anyone would in a job setting, you should either give her time off to manage the situation or let her go and find someone else. You don't ever want to put your child's well-being or safety at risk.

Suspected Abuse

If you suspect any sort of physical, emotional, or verbal abuse on the part of your nanny, you should terminate the relationship immediately. Some people will want to install cameras first and look for the smoking gun, but my strong advice is that if the act is hurting your child, *don't wait* to catch the nanny in the act. By doing so, you only expose your child to the risk of further harm. If you do decide to install cameras, make sure that you tell the nanny right away so that she knows she is being watched. This can help to ensure your child's safety while you look for someone new.

Whatever problems you may encounter with your nanny, you need to remember that there is always another nanny out there. If your current nanny situation is causing you stress, *don't be afraid to let her go* and search for someone better. We'll look more closely at how to part ways amicably and effectively in Chapter 12.

CHAPTER 11

———•———

I Love Her, but . . .

*Moms, Nannies, and the World's
Most Complex Emotional Bond*

Even when you've found the perfect nanny, the relationship between you will be unlike any other. You are the employer, and she is your employee, and yet the relationship is far more intimate than any you would ever have at an office. Because the nanny's workplace is your most private space—your home—she will likely, over the course of your time together, come to know more about you, your marriage, and your child than many of your closest friends. She will see you in your pajamas before you've brushed your teeth, she will witness your fights with your partner or spouse, and she will have a front-row seat when you make mistakes with your child and struggle not to doubt yourself as a parent. It's a very vulnerable situation for any mother to be in, and it's not surprising that many moms, even if they love their nanny, have mixed feelings about the arrangement. There is simply no way to bring another woman into your home—especially a woman whose job it is to love your child—and not have it stir up some complicated emotions from time to time.

I know from my own experience with my nanny, Maria, just how tricky these different emotions can be. When we first hired Maria, I felt tremendously guilty about having a nanny. After all, my mother had raised me and my sisters perfectly well without help from anyone other than my father. Furthermore, like so many new moms, I had a hard time gaining confidence as a parent, and Maria's skills and natural ease with Braydin seemed to confirm my worst fears and insecurities. She was better at remaining calm when Braydin cried, she was better at playing blocks, she was a better cook, and she woke up every morning smiling and singing Brazilian show tunes while I could barely function until I'd had my second cup of coffee. I genuinely worried that Maria was so good at mothering that Braydin would start preferring Maria to me. Everything that Maria did right with Braydin, and Braydin's obvious delight at being with her, sent me into a never-ending spiral of self-doubt.

I didn't know it then, but all of these emotions—and plenty of others too—are completely normal when you are one-half of a mother–nanny relationship. As time went on, I learned to stop measuring myself against Maria and to focus on all of the good things that she brought to our household. I realized that, far from undermining my role in the family, her presence actually allowed me to be a *better* mother. I could pursue my career *and* have quality time with my children and husband because she managed some of the domestic duties that would normally fall on my shoulders. Even now, she gives me the opportunity to have one-on-one time with each of our three girls, to actually be able to sit and listen, and to give them my full attention because I'm not simultaneously rushing to clean up the kitchen or keep the littlest one from smothering our cat. Instead, I can focus on my strengths as a parent and know that, even if there are some things I'm not as good at—like playing My Little Pony for hours on end or cooking up a gourmet feast—she is there to fill in any gaps with her expertise. As a result, my children are getting the best from us both, and I firmly believe that they will grow up happier for it.

This chapter explores some of the common emotions and fears that parents, especially mothers, may experience while having a nanny and offers some of my coaching strategies and practical suggestions for working through them. No matter what you may be feeling about your nanny, know that there are thousands of other mothers who feel exactly the same way, and that doing

> Doing the nanny–mom dance is never easy.

the nanny–mom dance is never easy. As a parent myself, I fully understand that it can be hard to watch another woman bond with and care for your child. But I also know that if you are lucky enough to employ a nanny, you have a rare opportunity to enhance and strengthen your entire family.

Mom Anxiety 1: I Should Be Doing More for My Child

Whether they work full-time or part-time or have chosen to be at home, almost every parent feels on some level that they should be doing more for their child. Working parents often feel guilty about leaving their children and that they cannot be there to share in every moment. I would point out, however, that just as many stay-at-home parents feel that they could or should be doing more. I had one mother who was at home full-time lament, "I feel like all I do is drag my children around on errands. I almost never sit down with them to play or read because there's always so much to do around the house." And I've had countless parents, both working and at home, confess, "I know that I should try to play more or do more creative things like crafts—but I just get so bored playing superheroes or coloring that I'd rather be doing anything else!"

Mothers everywhere are so hard on themselves. We feel so much pressure to be perfect at every single aspect of mothering and to make sure that our child eats the best food, has the best toys, goes to the best schools, and is perfectly entertained and stimulated for all of his waking hours. We chastise ourselves for losing patience, for being tired, for serving leftovers again, for buying the birthday cake rather than making one, and for not being as brilliant and creative as all of those millions of moms on Pinterest. But I always tell parents to remember my 100 ≠ 100 rule: *You cannot give 100 percent to your children 100 percent of the time.* No one can. It is physically and mentally impossible. You *need* to give some of yourself to your career, your marriage, your hobbies, your friends, and to activities—whether it's going to yoga or reading a magazine while your kids watch a video— that give you some mental breathing room and allow you to take a break. Motherhood is, by definition, a constant, never-ending endeavor: It is 24/7, all the time, week after week, year after year. If you don't take time for you and give yourself permission to occasionally give less, you will be exhausted, resentful, and certainly not your best self for your child.

Fortunately, that's where your nanny comes in. When you have a nanny, you are paying someone to step in and give your child 100 percent when you cannot because that's her job, and it's what she's trained to do. If you don't have the desire to play princesses or the energy to set up the easel and paints, your nanny is there to do those things with great enthusiasm so that your child isn't missing out. Nannies are able to give so much because, no matter how hard they work, they go off duty at the

> You cannot give 100 percent to your children 100 percent of the time.

end of the day. They don't have to be up in the night when your child is sick or lie awake worrying about Wednesday's math test or saving for college. When you have a good nanny, you have the luxury of knowing that even when you need to shift your focus elsewhere—either because you have to earn a living or because you simply need time for yourself—your child is still getting that 100 percent and experiencing that all-important Constancy of Care.

GETTING OVER IT

Whenever you feel like you are falling short, remind yourself that there is no one best way to be a mother and that what is best for someone else may not be best for you. You don't have to clean the house or cook all the meals or play all the games for your children to feel loved and to know that you—and only you—are Mom. If you want to do all those things, then that's great too, but there is *no rule* and no handbook for motherhood that says you have to do everything. Even the father of mother–infant attachment theory, John Bowlby, stated that parenting "is no job for a single person. If the job is to be well done and the child's principal caregiver not too exhausted, the caregiver herself (or himself) needs a great deal of assistance."* Sharing the responsibilities of parenting with your nanny *does not* make you less of a mother. In fact, by delegating some responsibility to her, you are ensuring that your child will always get what he needs.

Instead of giving in to this fear, take some time and write down a list of ways that you can use your nanny to be *more* of a mother. For

* John Bowlby, A *Secure Base: Parent-Child Attachment and Healthy Human Development* (New York: Basic Books, 1988), p. 2.

example: "I will take Gwendolyn to the library every week for story hour while the nanny stays home with the baby." "I will have the nanny do some of our errands during the week so that on Saturdays we can always spend the morning as a family." "While the nanny gives Jane her bath, I will spend quality time with Will, either helping with his homework or reading." "If the nanny bakes the birthday cake while I am at work, I can still frost it and decorate it just like Lizzie wants when I get home."

Chances are that your child will also benefit from whatever you do during your "me time," so instead of viewing your time apart as something that takes away from your child, try to focus on what it *gives* him. Working so that your child can have a home and food and opportunities in life *is* caring for him, and taking a break so that you can return to the home front happier and better able to engage with your child is giving him a gift as well.

Mom Anxiety 2: I Feel Guilty Just Having a Nanny

The biggest complaint that I hear from moms is that they feel guilty for having a nanny, period. Sometimes this is because they are sensitive about the class status that having a nanny implies, and sometimes they feel the guilt of privilege and are uncomfortable hiring someone from a different ethnic and possibly lower economic background to work in their home. Sometimes the guilt is imposed by the people around them, typically mothers or mothers-in-law who never had any help themselves and question—especially to moms who are at home—"What do you need a nanny for?" Even other mothers your own age may make subtle digs that make you feel like a nanny is a gratuitous luxury: "Oh, you don't have to do school dropoff because you have a nanny? Wow, you're lucky." These comments typically result from jealousy; they think that if you have a nanny, you must be sitting around eating bonbons all day or going to the spa in all your spare time, when nothing could be further from the truth.

Fathers can also contribute to mommy guilt. I can't tell you the number of dads who complain that the nanny is unnecessary, that it's a waste of money, and that it's not justifiable, especially if the mom is at home for some portion of the week. But in truth, no matter how involved and devoted your partner is, it is usually the mother who is on the front lines of parenting—whether that means breast-feeding round-the-clock after the baby is born, meeting with the teacher to discuss an issue at school, or rushing to sign up for the hard-to-get-into dance class. Until the father has truly walked in the mother's shoes—whether that means caring for the children 24/7 or arriving home after a long workday to start the second shift and make dinner and put the kids to bed—it is almost impossible for him to fully grasp how challenging and exhausting mothering can be. When he questions why you need the help and suggests that you should be managing on your own because his mother did it, or his friends' wives do it, he feeds that negative inner voice inside your head that wonders, "If I have a nanny, does that mean I'm lazy or overprivileged? Should I really be paying someone else to do my job?"

GETTING OVER IT

Whenever clients tell me that they feel guilty about having a nanny, the first question I ask them is, "*Who* is making you feel guilty?" and if they answer, "My mother," the next question I ask is, "Do you think she could have used a nanny?" They almost always answer,

"Hell, yes! She yelled at us all the time because she was overburdened and exhausted." If they say, "It's my mother-in-law" or "It's my husband," I ask, "Did your husband tell you that his mom was the perfect mother, always smiling and happy and fulfilled?" and they usually say something like, "No, she was bitter because she had no life beyond the kids."

The truth is that every mother in the world could benefit from another caring, capable adult to share childcare responsibilities, but not every family can afford it. Previous generations of mothers had more help because they lived close by to their parents, sisters, and aunts. Friends and neighbors helped each other out, and it was a village collectively raising a child. But today, those options usually don't exist, and as a result, we have an exceptionally taxed generation of mothers. While formulating his landmark theory of child development, John Bowlby spent time with African tribal communities and was struck by the tremendous level of support that the mothers had around them at all times. He concluded that the more support you have, the better mother you will be, and that your child will benefit greatly as a result.

Whenever mothers question whether they really need the nanny, I tell them to take the nanny out of the picture and imagine what it would be like without her day to day and then ask themselves, "Is it better?" If you had to wake your baby up and bring her out into the cold to take your older child to school or if you couldn't spend quality time with your children on the weekends because you had to do a week's worth of laundry and clean the house, who is winning in that scenario? In every case, when you take away the nanny, the mom may feel less guilty, but it is the child who will bear the burden. Sure, you can drive all the carpools and make dinner every day—there are plenty of moms who do it—but your child may not be getting the best of you as a result. You should also remind yourself that by having a nanny, you have given your child someone in addition to her parents who she loves and trusts, and this type of additional positive relationship, according to the science of child development, has been proven to create a happier, more confident, more resilient child.[*]

So yes, while a nanny is a luxury, she's not the same as a fancy car, or a $1,000 outfit—this is a luxury that will directly benefit your child if used in the right way. I had one mother who told me, "When I thought about what you said and realized that having a nanny was not about me, me, me, but ultimately about my daughter, all the negative voices stopped." Even the dads, after they stop protesting, usually find the nanny to be a huge help. I've had fathers call me back to apologize, admitting that the nanny was worth every penny because she made his wife happier and improved their marriage and household overall.

Mom Anxiety 3: My Nanny Does Everything Better Than I Do

Many moms, especially new ones, experience feelings of inadequacy when they compare themselves to their nannies. If you have a nanny who does everything perfectly—she keeps the house running smoothly and your child calm and happy—it can be easy to feel like you pale in comparison. Many moms begin to doubt their own parenting skills and wonder, "If the nanny is so great at caring for my child, what am *I* doing as a mother? What is my role in the family?"

Childcare is one of the only professions where an employee's success or expertise can affect her boss on such a deeply personal level. In my experience, if a nanny excels at her job, one of two things is

[*] Penelope Leach, *Childcare Today* (New York: Vintage Books, 2009), pp. 29–32.

going to happen: Either the mom and nanny will coexist in a harmonious, happy partnership or the mom will feel threatened and—either consciously or subconsciously—work to undermine the nanny and the relationship. I have seen numerous cases where mothers sabotaged the nanny because she was *too* good at her job or created fictional dramas so they could have an excuse to fire her. I was called into mediate between one of my clients and her nanny, and after the session, the nanny called me in tears, saying, "I just don't understand how I am working so hard, the children love me, and I'm doing everything well, but the mom is so unhappy with me. She yells at me and criticizes me all the time." When I pressed the mother to try to articulate what it was about the nanny that bothered her so much, she too broke down crying and said, "I've been a stay-at-home mom for ten years, and for a decade I have taken care of the house and done everything for my kids. If she's doing it all now, what is my role? What job am *I* supposed to do?"

When you put two women together in the same space and ask them to share the same responsibilities as well as the love of the same child, it is inevitable that comparisons will be made, and sometimes competition can result. As mothers, we all have in our minds an idealized version of the mother we would like to be, and it can be upsetting and even threatening when a nanny or another caregiver seems to get closer to that ideal than we do. In my own early years as a mom, I often saw Maria as the embodiment of everything I lacked domestically because she kept our household running in a calm and organized fashion that I just simply could not attain. One night, after I had gone out to see a client, I arrived home to find my daughters bathed, dinner on the table, cookies in the oven, and an entire play city made out of old cardboard boxes on the living room floor. I thought, "My God, I left to see one couple for sixty minutes—how on earth did she do all this in one hour, and why can't I do the same?"

These moments can really shake you as a mother, and make you question, "Is she a better mother than I am?"

A veteran nanny of twenty-five years once told me, "I like to be good at my job, but not so good that the mom begins to resent me." That may be a good strategy on the nanny's part, but if you feel competitive with your nanny or find yourself criticizing and critiquing her every move, ask yourself if you really want to create a home environment where the nanny feels that she can't be her best. If she can't bring her A-game for fear that you will become resentful, then both you and your children will be losing out. You owe it to yourself to fight the natural urge to make comparisons and to take advantage of every single talent, skill, and capability that your nanny has to offer.

GETTING OVER IT

First and foremost, you need to remember that caring for children is the nanny's *job*. It is her craft. She is supposed to excel at it, and that's what you are paying her for. It may not be *your* craft, but it doesn't have to be. Your craft may be consulting, or marketing, or being an academic, or whatever else you chose to pursue as a profession. Your child may have more fun playing Barbies with the nanny, but that's OK because nannies are paid to be professional Barbie players. You have your own inborn gifts and skills as a parent, some of which may become applicable or valuable only as your children grow and mature. I also tell parents to think about it this way: Your home is her office, and she is being paid to bring her best every time she walks through the door, just as you would bring your best when walking into a boardroom or an operating room.

The most important thing to remember is that your kids are not keeping track of who bakes more cookies or who plays trains better or tallying up "mom did this and the nanny did that." There is no score or report card at the end of this journey. The only one who is judging you is *you*.

So whenever you feel the urge to compare or doubt yourself, take a deep breath and quiet the negative voice in your head that whispers that the nanny is a reflection of what you are not. Then be proactive and focus on creating moments and experiences that *only* you and your child can share. A great way to do this is to come up with a few daily or weekend rituals that you can do together on a regular basis, such as reading before bedtime, making pancakes

> The only one who is judging you is *you*.

together on Saturday mornings, having chats before bed, or watching football on Sundays. At the end of the day, your child is far more likely to remember these rituals than he is to remember who did his laundry or packed his lunch.

Mom Anxiety 4: I Feel Like My Child Loves the Nanny More Than He Loves Me

Most mothers hope that their nanny and child will form a special, loving bond. But sometimes when it actually happens, they feel differently. If your child runs to the nanny first after he falls and scrapes his knee or cries when the nanny leaves at the end of the day but not when you leave to go to work, you may feel envious or replaced. The closer the nanny and your child become, the more tempted you may be to speculate about which one of you your child prefers.

Even as a clinician, it took some time for me to fully understand what made me and my nanny, Maria, different in the eyes of my children when we did many of the same things. We both loved them and snuggled them and gave them positive reinforcement; we took turns taking them to school and activities and the park; we both cared for them when they were sick and held them when they were upset. My youngest daughter even calls Maria "Mom-ia," which might be too much for some overly self-critical moms to bear.

But this I know without question, both from firsthand experience and years of research: There is no other person on the planet who can love a child as much as her own mother. So trust me when I say, there is only one Mom, and no one will ever take your place. Every single study in this area has shown that in the end children do not care about being with the best playmate or the best cookie maker or even the person who's around most of the time—in the end, all they really want is their mom. Also, it is a wonderful thing for a nanny to bond with your child. It means that you can leave to go to work or to a doctor's appointment and have your child feel calm and happy because there is someone who he trusts besides Mom and Dad. Studies also show that children with actively engaged parents *and* additional actively engaged caregivers have more confidence and trust in others at an earlier age, and this is something that will serve them well throughout their lives.* You don't want to be one of those mothers who can't use the bathroom or get a cup of coffee because her child is screaming and clinging to her leg. Some mothers like that because it makes them feel better to be the center of the child's world, but those children will struggle with separation down the road.

GETTING OVER IT

While I was writing an article, I once asked my oldest daughter to explain the difference between me and Maria, and she said, "I love playing in the basement with Maria, but I love just *being* with you.

---

* Penelope Leach, *Childcare Today* (New York: Vintage Books, 2009), pp. 29–32.

You made me, Mom, and you are my everything." We mothers often forget that we do not always need to be doing something to demonstrate that we are the best or to earn or keep our child's love. Worrying that the nanny is going to replace us is an irrational fear that has no basis in reality, and one that preys on a mother's greatest insecurity. After all, if this really happened, there would be millions of children out there who had abandoned their parents for the nanny, and as a clinician who spends her time talking to families and children who have nannies every day, I can assure that this just simply isn't the case.

Whenever you feel a twinge of jealousy, talk through your concern and then challenge it with the truth: "How on earth could this person really take my place?" and remember: You will *always* be Mom, today and every day, but your nanny will only be the nanny (and perhaps your child's favorite playmate) for just this short period of time. The clinical facts state that you can *never* surround a child with too much love, and the more love your child gives and receives, the happier, more confident, and well adjusted he will be. Now, whenever my daughter calls Maria "Mom-ia," instead of thinking, "She loves her just like she loves me," I see it as a beautiful representation of what Maria means to my daughter: a mommy when Mommy is not at home, and a "Maria" when she is. Her special name is proof that we have achieved Constancy of Care and that my daughter feels a parent's level of attention and affection even when I am not there. If your child truly loves your nanny, it does not mean that there is anything wrong with your parent–child bond; it means only that you have chosen your nanny well.

Mom Anxiety 5: I Feel Weird Paying Someone to Love My Child

A lot of mothers are unsettled by the fact that when it comes to child-care, you are essentially exchanging currency for love. They question the feeling behind the care that their child receives and wonder, "Does the nanny really love my son, or just the paycheck at the end of the week?" This mistrust and uncertainty can cause some moms to fixate on whether the nanny is doing a good enough job and spark the kind of nitpicking and emotional confusion that can lead to trouble in the relationship.

GETTING OVER IT

Instead of viewing the nanny as solely a purveyor of love, try to think of her as a teacher or educator. These people are also paid to care about, instruct, and shape our children as individuals, but we don't find it odd that they command a salary. Would you be worried about paying a tutor or piano teacher or the fact that your child's camp counselor earns money and doesn't just care for children out of the goodness of her heart?

Having known and worked with hundreds of nannies, I can tell you from experience that most of them do become genuinely attached and even fall in love with the children in their care. It's one of the many reasons that the mom–nanny relationship can be so complex. If you have ever experienced a deep emotional attachment to an endeavor or creation in your professional life, you can under-stand a little bit of what the nanny feels when she has been responsi-ble for a child every day, sometimes for years, and what she feels when the relationship comes to an end. Yes, nannies are paid professionals, but it is the bond with your child that elicits the love, not the money.

Mom Anxiety 6: I Feel Guilty That She's with My Children Instead of Her Own

Some mothers get very hung up on the fact that their nanny has her own children, either here in America or in another country. They fret over the idea of the nanny leaving her own kids, either in daycare or with a relative, and showering the attention and affection that should be rightfully theirs on a different child. This guilt can cause mothers to pull back and be reluctant to ask for what they need from the nanny. Because the nanny has already made the ultimate sacrifice, the moms don't want to ask her for more than is absolutely necessary.

GETTING OVER IT

A nanny is getting paid for what she does, and by earning a living, she is taking care of her children, just as you earn a living to provide for yours. While it is true that some nannies may miss their children, especially if they are far away, it usually does not affect their performance on the job. The best thing you can do is to pay the nanny fairly, treat her respectfully, and know that you are helping her care for her children by employing her. If you really love the nanny and have the means to remedy some of the injustice you feel, giving her a bonus of some extra vacation time, a plane ticket home to see her kids, or use of a computer so she can do FaceTime or Skype can help everyone feel more positive about the situation.

• • •

Whenever you experience any of these emotions, it can be helpful to verbalize them to your partner, your friends, fellow moms, and sometimes even to your nanny, depending on the kind of relationship you have. Talking it through and challenging your fears or negative thoughts can bring you to a more confident, peaceful place. Then do your best to go beyond the talking, and ask yourself, "What are the steps I can take right now to embrace my nanny, and use her presence to help me become the mother I want to be?"

Above all, know that you are not alone, and that there is no perfect nanny–employer relationship, just like there is no perfect mom, perfect marriage, or perfect family. A good relationship with your nanny takes time, effort, and occasionally the courage to confront your own feelings. But by working through these issues, you can come to a place of gratitude where you see your nanny for the gift that she really is—a gift not only for your child but also for you.

CHAPTER 12

———

When It's Not Working

How to Let a Nanny Go

Sometimes no matter what you do, the relationship between you and your nanny can't be fixed. It may take months for you to come to this realization, or a single event may suddenly bring the problem into focus. Even if your nanny hasn't done anything seriously wrong, you may still have a sense that she no longer meets your needs and decide to search for someone better. When this happens, it is important to know how to end the relationship effectively, amicably, and with a minimum of drama. This chapter provides guidance on how to ease the parting of ways and how to overcome the fear, faced by many parents, of letting go.

No-Fault Firing

Nanny–family relationships don't always end because of some major blowup or betrayal. Sometimes the nanny and the family simply outgrow each other, and both parties have a sense that it's time to move on. Your family's needs will evolve as your child grows and your circumstances change, and not every nanny will be able to adapt. Here are some of the reasons you may rightfully feel like your once ideal nanny no longer suits your family, along with strategies for moving on.

NANNY CANNOT ADAPT AS YOUR CHILD GROWS

Just as there are doctors who specialize in certain kinds of medicine, there are nannies who are better at different developmental stages in children. They may be wonderful with infants but unable to handle the energy or willfulness of toddlers, or they may be terrific with both infants and toddlers, but have a harder time relating to older children. If you have doubts about whether your current nanny still meets your child's developmental needs, it may be necessary to let her go and hire someone better suited to this particular phase in your child's life. Here are some warning signs to look for:

Infant → Toddler

Even if your nanny was amazing with your baby and loved singing, rocking, and going on walks, toddlerhood is a whole new experience. It is much easier to control the day with a baby because he can't walk or run away and doesn't talk back. If your nanny is frustrated or exhausted by your toddler, she may be stunting his development. You should replace your nanny if she:

- Prefers to stay inside when your toddler needs to be out walking, running, and exploring
- Does not have the calm and patience necessary to teach your child essential toddler lessons such as how to share, take turns, and handle the word *no*

- Loved the rigid structure of the infant day (naps here, bottle here, food here) and now cannot go with the flow; toddlers need more flexibility and freedom
- Will not take the time to teach letters, sounds, and words, which may possibly slow your child's speech development

Toddler → Preschooler

Preschoolers require more independence and a nanny who will stand back a bit rather than guiding them through everything. They also require more stimulation through books, learning, and arts and crafts as well as trying new activities and making new friends. You should replace your nanny if she:

- Prefers to do activities alone with your child rather than setting up playdates and arranging outings with other friends and nannies
- Doesn't want to take the time to read books
- Doesn't want to do arts and crafts because she doesn't want to make a mess

Preschool → School Age

School-age children require a nanny who can interact with teachers, can monitor and help with homework, and can first shuttle the kids to soccer, then to ballet, and still have dinner on the table. You should consider replacing your nanny if she:

- Cannot handle a busier, constantly changing schedule
- Refuses to help or cannot help with homework
- Is ineffective when handling situations with your child's teacher
- Is unable to guide your child in handling more complex social dynamics and relationships with friends

- Cannot manage or cope with the ever-changing emotions of a preteen

If you feel like your nanny is no longer meeting your child's emotional or developmental needs, you owe it to your child to find someone who can. Your nanny may also be feeling that the new parameters of the job are not for her, so letting her go may be best for everyone involved.

NANNY CANNOT ADAPT AS YOUR FAMILY GROWS

It is completely reasonable and understandable that a nanny who was amazing caring for your first child may be less enthusiastic and less equipped to do the job now that you have three. The nanny may openly state her unhappiness about the change or it may be obvious that she is struggling to get through the day. If you see that she is rattled, letting her duties slide, or she seems to have less patience with the children, the job may just be too much for her. There are plenty of nannies who are great with multiple kids, but you need to screen for that in the hiring process and find someone who is up for the job. If your children are particularly high energy and intense, or are spaced fairly close together (example: three under the age of three) and you recognize that they will be a lot for anyone to handle, adding a second nanny or an au pair may be a better choice.

YOUNGEST CHILD GOES TO SCHOOL

"What should I do now that my little one is in school?" is one of the most common questions I hear from parents. At first people think that there will be nothing for the nanny to do, but if the nanny wants to stay and you want to keep her, there are usually a multitude of non-child-related projects such as errands, cleaning, or organizing that the nanny can help with around the house. It can also be useful to have a second driver for after-school activities or someone to prepare dinner while you're transporting everyone around. If it's a monetary issue, and you can't afford both school and the nanny or you simply want to cut back on childcare expenses, you can see if the nanny is willing to do a nanny share or go part-time. Nannies usually know that this change is coming, so the best thing to do is sit down together and talk about it. If you don't want to keep her, there are ways that you can help her transition to a new position with another family as thanks for a job well done (see page 248).

MOM (OR DAD) WANTS TO STAY HOME

If you decide to leave your office job to either work from home or be at home full-time, you will first need to decide whether or not you want the nanny to stay. If you do, the next step is to have a conversation to see how she feels about the change in the home dynamic. Some nannies do not like working with moms at home because they feel that the moms micromanage them and undermine the control they have with the children.

For the transition to work, you and your nanny will need to be very honest with each other—and yourselves—about whether you can work together in the same space and bring out the best in each other rather than fighting for control. Even though you are Mom, you will have to respect the way that the nanny has run the house in your absence and work collaboratively with her to make any changes that fit the new mom-is-home arrangement. All of this can be easily done if you and your nanny communicate well and are willing to compromise. But if it's not working out and you and the nanny are at odds over everything and constantly stepping on each other's toes, then you may have to hire a new nanny who is more comfortable in a partner or executor role. If this is the case, the nanny will likely sense that her days are numbered. As with any nanny who has served you well and is leaving due to changed circumstances, it is good form to give her ample time and notice and to assist her in finding a new job.

CHANGE IN LOCATION

Many young families outgrow their small city apartments and want to bring their nanny with them when they move to a more suburban area. But often the change in surroundings and mobility, not to mention the commute, can be too much for the nanny to handle. City nannies, who are used to being autonomous and walking everywhere, often have the hardest time shifting to driving, suburban jobs. Changing the location of the nanny's home base and trying to shift the position from live-out to live-in can also exacerbate the issue; I have seen countless nannies who loved the children dearly and tried to shift to live-in when the family moved farther away, only to find that the overall change in circumstances was just too extreme, so they left.

If you know you are moving, you will need to think long and hard about whether it is a good idea to try to bring your nanny with you. Revisit and revise your FNA and think about how the parameters of your job will change, and then ask yourself—and ask the nanny—if she is truly capable of meeting your needs. Oftentimes it is better and easier in the long run to start fresh and hire someone new who lives closer, knows the area where you'll be living, has a manageable commute, and won't compare the job to the way it was before. If you gloss over the potential obstacles and then your nanny ends up quitting, you may be left in the lurch.

DIVORCE

As a therapist, I happen to believe that a good nanny can be invaluable during a divorce. She can take some of the pressure off the parents and help ease the transition by being a stable, consistent presence for the child. The key is to keep the nanny as neutral as possible rather than making her the ally of one parent or the other. To ensure that the nanny remains loyal to both parents, I usually have the parents pay the nanny jointly (even if one parent is actually paying the full amount) so that the nanny knows, "Both of these parents are my boss and I don't need to defer to one over the other. I should act impartial and focus solely on what is best for the children."

If you cannot keep your nanny during or after a divorce, it is best to make the change slowly if you can, because your children will experience a major shock if their parents separate *and* their trusted caregiver leaves. Do whatever you can to keep the nanny as long as possible and try to give her plenty of notice when you finally have to let her go.

PHYSICAL OR MENTAL ILLNESS OF A PARENT

If one parent is coping with a serious illness such as cancer or is struggling with a mental illness such as depression or addiction, you need a nanny who is willing and able to jump in and support the entire family. Some nannies are up to the challenge and will go above and beyond without a second thought; others will resent the change in home dynamics and responsibilities. If you have a nanny who draws a hard line, you should think seriously about replacing her with a new nanny who is open to doing more and can compensate for the suffering parent. I had one family where the mother was going through chemotherapy, and yet the nanny was complaining about having to do extra dishes. We replaced her with a more compassionate, understanding caregiver who could not only take care of the children but the mother as well.

If you or your partner is struggling with an illness, it is very important to discuss it openly with the nanny and ask her directly if she is willing to help. You should also be open to her input about how to best keep the household running during this time, and empower her to take charge and do whatever is necessary. If you feel that you cannot afford to keep your nanny due to mounting medical bills, be frank about the issue and see what she says; I have seen several nannies who were so loyal to the family that they agreed to work for reduced wages. I strongly recommend retaining some sort of childcare help if possible because in these rare situations the nanny is far more than a professional employee—she becomes a crucial emotional fixture that is necessary for the child's and sometimes the entire family's well-being.

FINANCIAL STRUGGLES

Families go through economic ups and downs, and sometimes the expense of a nanny is no longer possible. If this happens to you, don't lose heart—there are ways that you may be able to retain your nanny at a lower weekly rate. The first step is to explain your situation to the nanny and tell her that you will need to reduce her salary, and by how much. If you and the nanny both want to stay together, she may be open to doing a nanny share or to picking up extra hours with another family so that she doesn't experience a drop in pay. If your nanny agrees to either of these scenarios, you should help her find families who can be a source of additional income: Place an ad on a local posting board or email your friends to see if anyone needs help for a couple of hours a week.

Some nannies will not want to split their time and decide that they prefer to work elsewhere. If this is the case, you will need to respect her wishes and let her go. Sometimes a nanny will agree to continue working for you while she looks for another job, but even if she does, you should start your own search for a new nanny, or line up another form of childcare, such as daycare, as soon as possible.

HOW TO PART WAYS AMICABLY

If you are letting your nanny go due to a change in circumstances, you will want to end the relationship peacefully and professionally. If you really like the nanny and she has provided the Gold Standard of care for your child, helping her find her next job is a great way to pay her back for all that she has given your family during her years of service. Here are some ways to wind down the relationship on a positive note:

- **Give as much notice as possible.** If a nanny is not leaving your family for cause, two to four weeks' notice is standard, so that she can start her search for a new position while still earning income. If you're not in any rush, some nannies will agree to keep working right up until the day they start their new job.
- **Give severance.** Severance for nannies is typically one week's salary for every year of employment, but if you love the nanny and she has been an integral part of your family, it is good to be generous with the severance. Most nannies do not have a large financial cushion to fall back on and she will likely be worried about income. Whatever you can do to help her out until she finds another job will be greatly appreciated. I have seen employers give up to six months of

severance, pay for healthcare, or pay the next month's rent so the nanny does not have to worry about being evicted.

- **Write up a beautiful reference letter.** If you feel that your nanny deserves a good reference, give her a letter than she can share with other families. Your letter should state why you loved the nanny, what she did for your family, how long she was there, and how she connected with your children. Try to give specific, positive examples of ways that she impressed you or went above and beyond. You may also choose to state why she is leaving if you want to make it clear that the nanny is not at fault. Offer to speak to future families and provide your contact information.
- **Pass around her details** and contact information to friends, or post an ad for her on a website.
- **Give your child a chance to say good-bye.** Especially if the nanny has been with your family for a long time, make sure that you help

---

SAMPLE SEVERANCE LETTER

Date ___

This letter is to serve as proof of our termination of employment that began on ___ and will end on ___. It is agreed that you will be paid in full for your services up through the date of your departure. In addition, you will receive ___ weeks of severance in the amount of ___ as well as [rent, health insurance, or any additional nonmonetary item].

We appreciate the time that you worked for our family, and we wish you the very best in your professional endeavors. We know that you will find another family who is lucky to have you. All parties will sign below and agree to part ways amicably and with professional goodwill.

Signatures

your children transition by giving them a chance to say good-bye, give one more hug, or play their favorite game with her one more time. You should also make it clear to your child that he or she has nothing to do with the nanny leaving. Be as honest as you can about the reason—"She's leaving because we're moving and she can't come with us"—so that your child doesn't think, "Mabel left because she doesn't love us anymore."

- **Write and sign a severance letter.** Even if you are not firing for cause, it is a good idea to write a letter that spells out the details of the nanny's departure and severance so that there is no confusion later on. Be sure to date your letter, and have you, your partner, and your nanny all sign it on her last day so that, if necessary, she can file for unemployment.
- **Take care of administrative tasks.** Be sure that you take back your keys and credit cards and remove the nanny from any emergency contact lists or allowed pickup lists at school.

Firing for Cause

Firing for cause means that you are firing someone on account of what she has done or what she has failed to do, and it is a very different process from simply letting someone go due to a change in your family's needs or circumstances. When parents fire for cause, they typically end the relationship that same day because they no longer want the nanny in their home. There is usually no giving the nanny two weeks' notice or severance, and the conversation between the family and the nanny may be difficult or strained. It takes guts to truly fire someone, which is unfortunately why so many parents drag their feet even when it is clear that the nanny needs to go. However, if you really want what is best for your child, you should put your fears aside and act to get rid of the nanny as quickly as possible.

HOW TO FIRE A NANNY

Your goal when firing a nanny for cause is to extricate yourself from the relationship *as peacefully and professionally as possible*. Nannies don't always play by the same professional rules, and when they're fired, they may become hostile or lash out because they have nothing left to lose. I've had nannies who kept calling families, who wrote letters, who stalked the children, and who started all-out wars because they felt that they were treated poorly. You want to tread very, very carefully so that the situation doesn't turn into something ugly. Here's how to do it:

- **Take a deep breath and calm down.** Firing someone is a very sensitive, potentially explosive conversation, and nothing is gained by yelling or hysterics. Yes, you may be furious with the nanny. Yes, she may have broken your agreement. But there is *nothing* to be gained by yelling or threatening her or shaming her with extensive reprimanding; it can only escalate the situation. You want to do it as quietly and non-emotionally as possible.
- **Ask yourself, "Is this really what I want to do?"** If you're having last-minute doubts, ask yourself one more time, "Is there any possibility that this situation can improve?" If the answer is no and what the nanny has done is inexcusable or you've tried to address it with poor results, then you should move forward with confidence, knowing that you are doing the right thing.
- **Don't delve too deep into the reason for termination.** In my experience, drilling down on the nanny's failings will only cause tension and animosity, so while the nanny deserves to know the reason, it is better to keep your explanation short and simple. I had one client, a mom, who came home from work one day to find the nanny stepping out of the shower in the master bathroom, wearing the

mom's bathrobe with nothing underneath, and using the mom's hairbrush, which had been put away in her dresser drawer. Even though my client was horrified, she kept her cool, sent the nanny home, and then called her up later that night to fire her. Instead of ranting about the inappropriateness of the nanny's actions, she simply said, "We felt that today's situation was unprofessional" and ended the relationship with grace. If there are multiple reasons, or the overall situation just isn't working out, you can say something like, "Our needs have shifted and we've decided to make a change." Even if the reason is extremely serious, like stealing or physical abuse, it is better to let the nanny go without getting into it and then let the proper authorities handle the rest.

- **Fib if you have to.** If a nanny is off her baseline personality or if she has been acting strangely or having problems in her personal life, *do not* fuel the fire. If you need to tell a white lie to soften the blow and get her out of the house—such as, "My husband lost his job and we can't afford a nanny anymore"—then do it.

- **Decide whether or not to give severance.** Technically, you do not have to pay the nanny severance when terminating for cause. How-

> One nanny we hired was going through a divorce. We didn't think it would be an issue at the time, but as the proceedings became contentious, she became more and more unstable until one day she was arrested for domestic violence! I finally had to tell her that I was going to stay home full-time and we no longer had a position for her—which wasn't true, but I was worried that she'd totally lose her mind if I told her she was too unstable to work with my children.
>
> —SASHA, MIAMI, FL

ever, if the nanny is off balance or struggling emotionally, or you suspect that she is going to take it badly, you may want to provide some sort of severance to help de-escalate the situation. This is a case where paying it forward can protect you by facilitating a calm, professional parting of ways.

- **Write up a letter of termination.** It is a good idea to provide a formal letter of termination that both you and the nanny can sign so that there is no confusion about what has occurred. But again, *do not* get into the reason for termination or use the letter as an excuse to air dirty laundry. The nanny may think that this letter is something that the government will see or that other employers will see and that it is going to affect her for the rest of her life—and that alone could cause someone to flip out. In my opinion, there is no reason to put your nanny's faults on paper. All it does is put you at risk for someone acting inappropriately.
- **Do it at the end of the day** and when your children are not present. You should hand her the final payment (including any severance)

SAMPLE LETTER OF TERMINATION

Date ____
This letter serves as our formal termination letter. We are terminating your services on ____. You will be paid in full for the time you have worked for us and will receive a final payment of ____ [as well as severance in the amount of ____]. It is agreed by all parties that this letter shall serve to finalize the ending of our employment relationship from ____ to ____, and we agree to part ways in a professional manner.
Signatures

"BUT I CAN'T FIRE MY NANNY! WHAT ABOUT MY JOB?"

A lot of parents feel trapped because they know they need a new nanny, but they work full-time and the thought of being without childcare or conducting a nanny search from scratch is just too daunting. I have watched countless parents choose to overlook major problems and, against all logic, struggle on with mediocre or even terrible nannies because they think, "My job is too important, I can't miss work." To which I say: Get over it! Yes, you may be working and that's unfortunate, but unless you're saving lives or solving the Middle East peace crisis, you can take a day or two to get your nanny situation under control. Sometimes people have to miss work for personal reasons, and when you're talking about the well-being of your child, you need to make it your top priority. Here are some ways that you can give yourself enough bandwidth to fire your nanny and find someone new, even if you're working:

1. If you went through my Gold Standard hiring process, you know that having backup childcare is always essential for working parents. Now is the time to use it. Call up your parents, or babysitter, or your drop-in daycare center and arrange for them to look after your child so that you can fire your current nanny and look for a new one.

2. If you do not have backup childcare already in the wings, search the Internet for "emergency sitting services" or "on-call babysitting services" and try to find someone who can take your child for a few days or a couple of weeks until you sort things out.

3. Talk to your friends who have nannies. Is there someone who would be willing to do a nanny share for a few weeks until you can find and hire someone new?

4. Use your trials with new nannies as coverage. I had one client who wanted to fire her nanny as soon as possible, so we

arranged her search in such a way that the trials became her coverage. Before she let the nanny go, she spent time in the evenings sourcing candidates and doing screening and reference checks. She then took a Saturday to do all of the interviews, and then set up one-week trials with three different candidates. When she finally fired the nanny, she had three straight weeks of coverage already lined up, and she ultimately picked the new nanny she liked best.

The key to jump-starting the process is to say to yourself, "I'm not going to be frozen by the fact that I'm working; I'm really going to start trying to find someone new." Then you take it one step at a time. Send out an email to friends and colleagues to see if they have anyone to recommend, register with an agency, or browse postings online. Do your screening and reference checks at night after your nanny leaves. Do your interviews at night and on the weekends, and then take a day or two off from work for trials, or do them on the weekend. It is entirely possible to find and hire a new nanny without ever missing a day on the job.

---

and termination letter. If you are concerned about safety, ask a neighbor or your doorman, or hire a security person, to help you escort her from the premises.

- **Take care of administrative tasks.** Be sure to get any keys and credit cards back from the nanny before she leaves. You should also change your locks and security codes and remove the nanny from emergency contact lists as well as allowed pickup lists at school.

When Your Nanny Wants to Leave

If your nanny comes to you and says that she wants to leave, first try to find out why and see if the issue is something that you can fix.

Sometimes nannies will threaten to quit if they feel that they are being treated unfairly rather than simply approaching the parents to discuss the problem. If you like the nanny and you want her to stay, hear her out and then decide if you are willing and able to make changes. If you can't, see if she can give you one or two weeks rather than walking right out the door. I don't recommend that you push for more time because, in my experience, after a week or two the relationship begins to sour, and you do not want someone disgruntled and unhappy around while you are interviewing and trialing new nannies.

Above all, *do not ever force your nanny to stay* until you find a new nanny or threaten her in a way that makes her feel like she will get into legal trouble by resigning. I have seen parents point to their Nanny–Family Work Agreement and tell the nanny that she is bound to stay by contract, and I even had one mother, who was a lawyer, tell the nanny that she was obligated by law to keep working for them until they hired someone else. This poor nanny had no idea about employment law and was very afraid of getting into trouble, so the family exploited that fear and held her as a virtual prisoner in their home. *You cannot ever force an employee to continue working against her will.* A work agreement is not legally binding, and your nanny—just like any other employee in any profession—is entitled to quit and leave without giving notice at any time. In addition, because of the sensitive nature of the job, you never want an unhappy or resentful nanny in your home.

What to Tell Your Children

Sometimes a nanny leaves a family for concrete reasons, such as a move, that children can easily understand. But if you fire your nanny for cause or decide to end the relationship because your needs have changed or the nanny is no longer able to do the job well, you should avoid discussing the reason with your child. It almost never helps a child to hear bad things about the nanny, especially if they shared a special bond. Most young children are not capable of understanding why you got rid of someone they loved. I usually advise parents to say that someone in the nanny's family needs her (perhaps her child or a parent) because they are sick, and she had to leave immediately because she needs to help them. This way the children can understand and know that *it has nothing to do with them.*

If your children loved the nanny and she left on good terms, you can help them grieve the loss by drawing pictures of the nanny, writ-

---

SHOULD YOUR EX-NANNY HAVE CONTACT WITH YOUR CHILD?

If the nanny left your family on good terms, there is nothing wrong with staying in touch. I have seen cases where the nanny continued to send birthday cards to the children or even returned many years later to attend the child's wedding. As long as everyone is comfortable with the arrangement, you can continue the relationship in any way you choose.

If, however, you fired the nanny for cause or parted ways on bad terms, you are under no obligation to have any further contact. I have seen several cases where an ex-nanny sought out the children in places she knew they went, like the local playground, and I even had one case where the ex-nanny stopped by the house when the parents were not there and asked the new nanny if she could see the kids. No matter how upset the nanny was to leave your family, this kind of behavior is totally inappropriate, and if it occurs, you will need to call the nanny and tell her that she is to have no further contact. You should also make your new nanny aware of the situation and empower her to keep the former nanny away from your kids.

---

ing letters to the nanny, or even having the nanny come back and visit from time to time. If you fired the nanny for cause and she had to leave without saying good-bye, some parents have the child write a letter to the nanny and then write a pretend letter back that says, "Dear Sammy, I miss you so much. I loved taking care of you, but I had to go home to help my mother, who is sick. I am sending you hugs. Love, _____"

Whatever happens, *don't* let yourself feel trapped in a lackluster or unacceptable situation and fall into a pattern of paralysis. If your and your child's needs aren't being met, and you've tried addressing the issue through training and nanny speak to no avail, or if the nanny's behavior suggests any sort of duplicitousness or aggression, the only reasonable solution if you really want what's best for your family is to let the nanny go and hire someone else. As I've counseled so many other families who were in your shoes: Your family will be fine, your kids will be fine, and there are brighter days ahead.

> Your family will be fine, your kids will be fine, and there are brighter days ahead.

I know from experience that the world is full of wonderful nannies who are eager to have a true working partnership with a good family and are full of love to give to your child. With this book, you have everything you need to find that amazing person. I wish you, your child, and your nanny many happy years of success.

ACKNOWLEDGMENTS

I would not have been able to write this book without:

My Secure Base, Jason: If everyone had someone like you as their husband or father, all of us therapists would be out of work. Your selflessness, patience, and extreme devotion to our family is astounding. Through blissful highs and crushing lows you have always held the boat steady, helping me find the rainbow over the horizon. You taught me more than any teacher and your unwavering support and respect helped teach our girls gender equality and why they deserve nothing less. Most of all, you helped me create a happy home filled with daily laughter, joyful chaos, and unbreakable positivity. Jason, you made it all happen; you are not that missing piece—you're everything I dreamed of and more . . .

My First Princess, Braydin: Determined, graceful, and wise; already a compassionate mini-therapist sophisticated beyond her years. **My Angel Face, Picoley:** Who broke the "unhappy middle child" theory with her sparklingly sweet soul made of rainbows and butterflies. **My Littlest Lion, Gemma:** So fierce and fearless yet deliriously happy; a radiant child who literally jumps her way through life . . . Girls, thank you for sharing me during this process. I know sometimes it took me away from you, but I actually wrote this book because of you. In 2008, the economy went crazy and I worried about the future impact on you. I decided to create some additional projects in effort to support and protect your future dreams. This book is an example of those efforts and the lessons I share daily: "Work hard, think outside of the box, and turn negatives into positives." Nothing could derail the happiest and most important mission in my life—helping three magical little girls evolve into happy, healthy, and confident young women.

My parents, Pat and Phil: Thank you for your unconditional love and support as parents and grandparents and for planting the seed within me to work hard, never give up, and always use my voice. Without you, that snail would have never made it to the Ark . . .

My sisters, Heidi and Ilana, and my entire extended family: Thank you for always supporting and taking care of me and for making the happy events in life that much sweeter.

My pals: From Mendham to the Penn Posse to the NJ Mommies, I feel so lucky to have had so many wonderful women in every stage of my life. The kind of friends you see in movies, who always support you, stand by you, and love you exactly as you are. There are too many of you to name, but you know who you are and how much I love you.

My Fairy God-Manager, Wendy: Thank you for helping me build most of my nanny business with your eternal faith in my capabilities. You were the one who always knew I did much more than feed the elephants . . .

My right-hand lady, Jill Jensen: I cannot thank you enough for all of your invaluable help and for affording me the ability to stay with my children while you ran the business. Who would believe that I dictated this entire book to you while we were halfway across the country and during my endless trips to ballet, gymnastics, and Chuck E. Cheese's?

My agent, Andrea Barzvi: Thank you for taking a chance on me and for believing so deeply in this book.

My brilliant book partner, Ann Campbell: Thank you for transforming my highly clinical words into readable content beyond my dreams! I am honored to have worked with such an incredible talent.

My editor, Marian Lizzi: Thank you for giving me this opportunity and for being such a gracious editor. I am eternally grateful.

My clients: Thank you for sharing your lives with me and for trusting me.

My nannies: Sometimes without appreciation or recognition, in the blazing sun and freezing cold you are the nameless, faceless heroes who love and protect our children. My hope is that this book will give your important profession the respect and validation it deserves.

My Gold Standard, Maria: This book was based on you, Maria! You are the perfect nanny who improves the lives of children and parents every day. If all nannies could be as positive, patient, devoted, and loving, every family would be stronger, happier, and healthier. You are one of the hardest working and most dedicated people I have ever met, and I am a better mother and my children are happier people because we had you in our lives. I could never write a book big enough to thank you for caring for our family as if it was your very own. We love and are forever grateful to our beloved Mom-ia.

To my hero, Dr. John Bowlby: Your parents' loss is humanity's gain . . .

———•———

Family Needs Assessment

Part 1: Physical Job Description

1. Days for this position:

2. Hours for each day:

3. Preferred start date:

4. Where do you need your nanny to live? (Circle one.)

   Live-Out   Live-In   Combination

5. If this is a live-out position:

   • How far away can the nanny live?

   • Will you provide any transportation to and from your home or will the nanny be responsible for getting there?

   • Is there public transportation close to your home?

   • Will you provide a monthly pass or anything else to cover the cost of her transportation?

   • Would you provide a cab or car service home for the nanny if she has to work late at night (instead of requiring her to use public transportation)? If so, after what time at night would you provide this?

- Will there be any times when you need your nanny to live-in (for example, during vacations or while you are traveling for work)?

6. If this is a live-in position:
    - What accommodations will be provided for the nanny?

    - How will meals work? (For example, will she eat with the family even when she is not working? Will she be allowed to use the kitchen to prepare her meals?)

    - Will the nanny be required to assist with the children during the night or on the weekend? If so, how will she be compensated for that time?

7. Do you need your nanny to drive?

8. If your nanny will be driving . . .
    - Will she have use of a vehicle or will she need to provide her own car?

    - Will she be covered by your car insurance or will she need to provide her own?

    - If she is using her own car, will you provide money for gas or reimbursement based on mileage?

9. Does your nanny need to know how to swim?

  • If you find a great nanny but she doesn't swim, would you be
    willing to pay for swimming lessons?

10. Would you like your nanny to speak a second language, and if so,
    what?

  • How would you like her to use the language in your home?

11. Will your nanny need to be able to travel?

12. If you said yes to travel . . .

  • How often will the trips take place?

  • How long will the trips last?

  • During travel, what will the nanny's weekday and weekend
    pay rates be?

13. Are there any other benefits or perks you will provide?

Part 2: Job Duties and Responsibilities

1. What type of nanny are you looking for? (Circle one.)

   Parental unit nanny   Partner nanny   Executor nanny

2. What will be your nanny's *child-related* duties and responsibilities? (Check all that apply and list any additional ones.)

☐ Wake children
☐ Prepare bottles
☐ Bottle feedings
☐ Sterilize baby bottles
☐ Wash baby bottles
☐ Wash/sterilize pacifiers
☐ Wash/sterilize toys
☐ Tidy playroom
☐ Pick up toys
☐ Tummy time
☐ Plan meals
☐ Prepare meals
☐ Serve meals
☐ Clean up kitchen after
   meals
☐ Pack school lunches
☐ Dress children
☐ Wash children's laundry
☐ Fold/put away clothes
☐ Organize closets
☐ Diaper changes
☐ Restock diapers and wipes
☐ Restock diaper bag
☐ Empty diaper pail
☐ Bath
☐ Tidy bathroom after bath

☐ Tidy bedroom
☐ Child-related errands
☐ Doctor's visits
☐ Listen to music
☐ Plan activities/playdates
☐ Take to activities/playdates
☐ Indoor play
☐ Outside play
☐ School dropoff
☐ School pickup
☐ Unpack backpacks
☐ Homework
☐ Read
☐ Tutoring
☐ Work with teachers
☐ Work with therapists
☐ Organize sports equipment
☐ Buy gifts for birthday
   parties
☐ Create a schedule
☐ Maintain specified
   schedule
☐ Manage calendar
☐ Daily communication log
☐ Bedtime

☐ Additional:

3. If you have a child with special needs, are there any additional duties and responsibilities that the nanny will have regarding this child?

4. Are there any healthcare duties that must be performed for any of the children on a regular schedule?

5. What additional *household* duties do you wish the nanny to perform? (Check all that apply and list any additional ones.)

☐ Family laundry   ☐ Bring in newspaper
☐ Fold and put away clothes   ☐ Take out trash
☐ Family dishes   ☐ Take out recycling
☐ Make all beds   ☐ Wipe down counters
☐ Change sheets   ☐ Clean out refrigerator
☐ Tidy main living areas   ☐ Organize pantry
☐ Windows   ☐ Organize all closets
☐ Bathrooms   ☐ Organize entry areas
☐ Vacuuming   ☐ Organize mail
☐ Mopping   ☐ Run errands
☐ Sweeping   ☐ Dry cleaning
☐ Empty wastebaskets   ☐ Be at home to meet and
☐ Dust   manage housekeeper,
☐ Maintain grocery list   plumber, electrician, etc.
☐ Grocery shopping   ☐ If live-in, clean and
☐ Bring in mail   maintain own living area

☐ Additional:

6. If the nanny is required to cook, what will her specific cooking duties be?

7. Do you observe any religious dietary laws or have any dietary restrictions/preferences that the nanny must follow while in your home?

8. If driving is involved in the job, what are the driving duties required?

9. If there are pets in your home, will the nanny be required to care for them? If so, what duties are required?

   • Will the nanny be required to look after the house or pets if you go away for a period of time?

10. Describe a day in the life of your nanny, from the moment she starts in the morning until the end of the day.

11. Describe a worst-day scenario in your home.

12. Based on all of your previous answers, are there any specific skills that a nanny must have to effectively fulfill her duties and support each child?

Part 3: Emotional Job Description

A. PARENT ASSESSMENT (ANSWER THE FOLLOWING QUESTIONS FOR EACH PARENT)

1. How would you describe your parenting style?

2. How do you typically interact and communicate with your children?

3. Are you looking for someone to (check one and answer the questions that follow):

   ☐ Replicate your style completely

   • What in particular do you need her to replicate?

   ☐ Partner fifty–fifty in terms of style (that is, follow your lead but make her own contributions where appropriate)

   • In what ways do you want her to be like you?

   • In what areas can she take the lead?

   • Is there anything specific that you would prefer she do differently?

   ☐ Bring her own style and approach

   • What type of style and approach would you like her to have?

4. Are there any specific positions on childrearing that you would like your nanny to have or not have?

5. Have you ever employed a childcare provider before?

   • If yes, what worked well?

   • What did not work well?

6. Are there any practices or behaviors that are Deal-Breakers for you? What are the things that you feel strongly that your nanny *not* do?

7. Do you mind if your nanny has young children of her own?

8. Based on all of your answers in Section A, list the personal qualities and characteristics that you are most looking for in a nanny:

B. CHILD ASSESSMENT (ANSWER THE FOLLOWING QUESTIONS FOR EACH CHILD)

9. Using the chart beginning on page 74, what are your child's current developmental needs?

   • What specific skills and personality traits will a nanny need to have in order to meet these needs?

   • How will these needs change a year from now? In two years?

10. Describe the caregiver personality best suited to your child:

11. If your child is older, how does he or she feel about hiring a new nanny?

   • How do you think this may affect your nanny search and your ability to find and hire the right candidate?

   • Are there any steps that you can take to minimize how these feelings influence your search?

C. YOUR IDEAL NANNY

12. What does the ideal candidate look like for your family?

   Age:

   Experience:

Education:

Cultural background:

Language skills:

Personality:

Communication style:

Appearance:

Religion:

13. What are the best aspects of the position and working for your family?

14. What do you think will be the most difficult aspects of the position and working for your family?

15. What may be difficult for a new nanny coming into your home, and what skills might help the nanny with this transition?

Part 4: Summing Up

1. Based on all the information you've gathered from the previous questions, list the Must Haves for your job. These are the nanny skills, traits, and abilities that you can't live without. I recommend breaking them down into physical Musts (Parts 1 and 2) and emotional Musts (Part 3).

2. Now list the Pluses—skills and abilities that would be nice to have, but are not essential.

3. And finally, list your Deal-Breakers. These are the traits and habits that you cannot accommodate, no matter what. They should immediately disqualify any candidate who possesses them or who is revealed to possess them during the search process.

INDEX

Job duties, 16–17, 122
additional household, 61–63
cooking, 64
dietary restrictions and preferences,
64–65
driving, 65
of executor nanny, 26
healthcare, 60–61
household scenarios, 61–62
list of child-related, 58–59
nanny type, 58
normal day description, 65–66
of parental unit nanny, 25
of partner nanny, 25–26
pet care, 65
sharing in mother–nanny relationship,
227–28
skills requirement, 67–68
special needs child and, 60
worst day description, 66–67

Litmus test, 210
Live-in nanny, 18
accommodations, 52
advantages, 19
food situation with, 52–53
hours, 53
personality, 20
Live-out nanny, 18
commuting, 51
live-in times, 52
reliability, 20–21
transportation reimbursement, 51
Lying, 212–13
big lie confrontation, 219
consequences, 216
little, big and medium, 212
little lie confrontation, 217–18
medium lie confrontation, 218–19
needs compromised, 215–16
pattern of deception, 215
premeditation, 215
reasonableness of, 214

Maids, 34
Mary Poppins, 16
Medicine log, 164

Mistakes, addressing. *See also*
Communication
defensiveness and, 190–91
excuses, 191
nanny speak formula, 190
repeat occurrence, 191–92
thoughts about, 192
timing choices, 188–90
Mom Anxiety
on doing more for child, 225–28
fathers causing, 229
loves nanny more, 234–36
"me time," 228
motherhood definition, 226
nanny does better, 231–34
nanny guilt, 228–31
nanny's own children, 238
100 ≠ 100 rule, 226
paying to love child, 237–38
support needed, 230–31
Mommybites.com, 90
Mother–nanny relationship
better mother due to, 224
common emotions and fears, 225–39
competition, 232–33
differences, 234–36
emotional attachment, 237–38
inadequacy feelings, 231–32
intimacy, 223
jealousy, 236
judgment, 233–34
nanny's own children and, 238
self-doubt, 224
sharing responsibilities, 227–28
Musts
confirmation in screening steps, 94
in emotional job description, 85–86
emotional sample questions, 111
matching in Gold Targeted Check,
107–8, 109
physical sample questions, 110

Nannies. *See also* Executor nanny; Ideal
nanny; Live-in nanny; Live-out nanny;
Parental unit nanny; Partner nanny
advantage of having, 17
agencies, 88–89

ABOUT THE AUTHOR

Tammy Gold is a licensed therapist, certified parent coach, and founder of Gold Parent Coaching. As a nationally recognized parenting expert, Tammy appears regularly on *Good Morning America*, *The Today Show*, Fox, and CBS News. She has also appeared in more than 100 magazines and writes regularly for the *Huffington Post*, MommyCoach.com, TheBump .com, and Howcast.com. Tammy has worked with families and nannies for more than a decade, while also running parenting groups and giving lectures. Her Nanny Whisperer communication techniques were created from her work counseling couples, and her Gold Standard hiring process is based on Dr. John Bowlby's attachment theory, Erik Erikson's stages of child development, and Mary Ainsworth's secure base. Tammy is one of the first therapists to bring traditional psychotherapy tools to the process of finding and enhancing childcare. She earned her undergraduate degree from the University of Pennsylvania and her graduate degree from Columbia University. She lives in Short Hills, New Jersey, with her husband, Jason, and three daughters, Braydin, Presley, and Gemma.